Qualifications and Credit Framework (QCF)
LEVEL 4 DIPLOMA IN ACCOUNTING

TEXT

Option Paper:
Personal Tax
FA2009

2010 Edition

First edition July 2010

ISBN 9780 7517 8570 8

British Library Cataloguing-in-Publication Data
A catalogue record for this book is available from the British
Library

Published by

BPP Learning Media Ltd
BPP House
Aldine Place
London
W12 8AA

www.bpp.com/learningmedia

Printed in the United Kingdom

CONTENTS

Introduction   (v)

Assessment Strategy   (vii)

Study Guide   (ix)

Tax tables   (xii)

1   The Tax Framework   1

2   Employment income   11

3   Property income   39

4   Taxable income   53

5   Calculation of income tax   65

6   Self-assessment of income tax   75

7   Computing capital gains tax   87

8   Chattels and private residences   101

9   Shares   111

Answers to chapter tasks   119

Test your learning – answers   135

Index   149

A NOTE ABOUT COPYRIGHT

INTRODUCTION

This is a time of great change for the AAT. From 1 July 2010 the AAT's assessments will fall within the **Qualifications and Credit Framework** and most papers will be assessed by way of an on demand **computer based assessment**. BPP Learning Media has reacted to this change by investing heavily to produce new ground breaking market leading resources. In particular, our **new suite of online resources** ensures that students are prepared for online testing by means of an online environment where tasks mimic the style of the AAT's assessment tasks.

The BPP range of resources comprises:

- **Texts**, covering all the knowledge and understanding needed by students, with numerous illustrations of ' how it works', practical examples and tasks for students to use to consolidate their learning. The majority of tasks within the texts have been written in an interactive style that reflects the style of the online tasks the AAT will set. Texts are available in our traditional paper format and, in addition, as E books which can be downloaded to your PC or laptop.

- **Question Banks**, including additional learning questions plus the AAT's practice assessment and a number of other full practice assessments. Full answers to all questions and assessments, prepared by BPP Learning Media Ltd, are included. For the first time our question banks are available in an online environment which mimics the AAT's testing environment. This enables you to familiarise yourself with the environment in which you will be tested

- **Passcards,** which are handy pocket sized revision tools designed to fit in a handbag or briefcase to enable students to revise anywhere at anytime. All major points are covered in the passcards which have been designed to assist you in consolidating knowledge

- **Workbooks,** which have been designed to cover the units that are assessed by way of project/case study. The workbooks contain many practical tasks to assist in the learning process and also a sample assessment or project to work through.

- **Lecturers' resources**, providing a further bank of tasks, answers and full practice assessments for classroom use, available separately only to lecturers whose colleges adopt BPP Learning Media material. The lecturer's resources are available in both paper format and online in E format.

This Text for Personal Tax has been written specifically to ensure comprehensive yet concise coverage of the AAT's new learning outcomes and assessment criteria. It is fully up to date as at June 2010 and reflects both the AAT's unit guide and the practice assessment provided by the AAT.

Each chapter contains:

- clear, step by step explanation of the topic

- logical progression and linking from one chapter to the next

- numerous illustrations of 'how it works'

- interactive tasks within the text of the chapter itself, with answers at the back of the book. In general, these tasks have been written in the interactive form that students will see in their real assessments

- test your learning questions of varying complexity, again with answers supplied at the back of the book. In general these test questions have been written in the interactive form that students will see in their real assessments

The emphasis in all tasks and test questions is on the practical application of the skills acquired.

If you have any comments about this book, please e-mail suedexter@bpp.com or write to Sue Dexter, Publishing Director, BPP Learning Media Ltd, BPP House, Aldine Place, London W12 8AA.

ASSESSMENT STRATEGY

Personal Tax is the first of two tax assessments at Level 4. Assessments should be available from November 2010.

The assessment is normally a two hour computer based assessment.

The Personal Tax assessment consists of twenty-three tasks, fourteen in Section 1 and eight in Section 2.

Section 1 covers:

- General tax
- Employment income
- Investment, savings and dividend income
- Payment of tax
- Tax returns

There are twelve objective tasks and two extended tasks requiring a written response.

Section 2 covers:

- Property income
- Capital gains tax

There are eight objective tasks and one extended task requiring a written response.

Competency

Learners will be required to demonstrate competence in both sections of the assessment. For the purpose of assessment the competency level for AAT assessment is set at 70 per cent. The level descriptor in the table below describes the ability and skills students at this level must successfully demonstrate to achieve competence.

QCF Level descriptor	**Summary**
	Achievement at level 4 reflects the ability to identify and use relevant understanding, methods and skills to complete tasks and address problems that are well defined but complex and non-routine. It includes taking responsibility for overall courses of action as well as exercising autonomy and judgement within fairly broad parameters. It also reflects understanding of different perspectives or approaches within an area of study or work.
	Knowledge and understanding
	■ Practical, theoretical or technical understanding to address problems that are well defined but complex and non routine
	■ Analyse, interpret and evaluate relevant information and ideas
	■ Be aware of the nature and approximate scope of the area of study or work
	■ Have an informed awareness of different perspectives or approaches within the area of study or work
	Application and action
	■ Address problems that are complex and non routine while normally fairly well defined
	■ Identify, adapt and use appropriate methods and skills
	■ Initiate and use appropriate investigation to inform actions
	■ Review the effectiveness and appropriateness of methods, actions and results
	Autonomy and accountability
	■ Take responsibility for initiating and completing tasks and procedures, including, where relevant, responsibility for supervising or guiding others
	■ Exercise autonomy and judgement within broad but generally well-defined parameters

STUDY GUIDE

Personal tax

Introduction

For the purpose of assessment the Principles of Personal Tax (Knowledge) and Calculating Personal Tax (Skills) will be combined. Please read this document in conjunction with the standards for the unit.

The purpose of the unit

The general purpose of these units is to enable learners to understand the impact and significance of taxation on individuals. All sources of income for individuals, such as employment income, capital gains, income from land and property and investment income are covered. By studying these taxes, learners can appreciate the tax implications for their own personal situation, and that of colleagues and clients.

Learning objectives

On completion of these units the learner will be able to:

- demonstrate knowledge of how income tax and capital gains tax is applied to income

- calculate the income tax liabilities of an individual

- calculate income from all sources and apply relevant allowances, deductions and reliefs to prepare accurate income tax computations

- calculate the individual liability for capital gains tax

Learning outcomes

This unit consists of 9 learning outcomes. The learner will:

(1) demonstrate an understanding of legislation and procedures relating to personal tax.

(2) understand the current taxation principles of income from employment

(3) understand the current taxation principles of savings, non savings and dividend income for an individual.

(4) understand the current taxation principles of property income for an individual.

(5) understand the current principles of basic capital gains taxation for an individual.

(6) calculate income from all sources accurately.

(7) calculate accurately the tax payable on income.

(8) account for capital gains tax correctly

(9) prepare accurate computations and complete the relevant parts of the self assessment tax returns correctly.

Delivery guidance

General tax issues

This area underpins all the other specific taxation areas assessed within this unit. It should not be seen in isolation as, for instance, the Finance Act being assessed is relevant throughout the standards.

Documentation that needs to be kept by all parties is relevant here. Both the responsibilities of the taxpayer and the tax practitioner are relevant, in particular what documents need to be kept and for how long. The responsibilities of the tax practitioner are particularly important when handling client tax affairs and learners must be able to show understanding of this.

Additionally, learners will need to show understanding of the implications on taxpayers if full, accurate and timely disclosure of all tax related information is not provided to HRMC. The tax practitioner's role in this area should also be understood.

Employment income

Calculations of employment income, including various assessable benefits in kind are a crucial area of these standards. However, it is also expected that students will be able to explain this income in terms of providing basic advice to tax payers. For instance, being able to explain how job related accommodation operates is as relevant as being able to compute this benefit.

In addition, the learner must be able to show understanding of the impact of exempt benefits in kind. This should be from an operational perspective as well as giving either tax payers or companies advice on how to effectively use exempt benefits.

Property income

Income from property is an important aspect of income tax, and learners must be able to show knowledge of such income from a variety of sources. Furnished and unfurnished property, rent a room schemes, holiday lets and buy-to-let investments are all assessable. Computation of both rental income and the expenses that apply is important.

In addition, learners must be able to apply the rules for any losses made arising from these sources of income.

Other income

This will mainly apply to investment income, such as bank interest, building society interest, National Savings investments, and dividends. Some exempt income, such as interests from ISA's will also need to be understood.

Payment of tax

Under this heading, learners will need to be able to collate all income taxable under income tax and apply the rules for different bands and rates. For instance, how the 10% band on savings income applies, and how to treat the tax deducted at source from dividends will need to be understood.

An understanding of the payments on account system is expected, including when payments are due and how to pay them.

The impact of pension payments, both occupational and private, will need to be understood. Such knowledge will be restricted to the computational impact of these payments. Learners will not need to understand the complexities of pension payments, such as annual allowances and lifetime allowances. However, the extension of the basic rate will need to be understood. Also, learners should be able to explain the differences between occupational and private payments, providing basic advice to tax payers on these differences.

The impact of charity giving also needs to be understood. Giving through employment and direct gift aid needs to be understood, including the differences in how tax relief is obtained. Extension of the basic rate applies also here.

Taxpayers from the age of 16 are assessable and learners need to understand how personal allowances apply for different ages. This includes the income limit for age-related allowances. However, all references to married couple's allowances are not assessable, neither is the blind person's allowance.

In addition to this, learners need to understand the rules for penalties, surcharges and interest as they apply to payment of tax, posting of tax returns and filing of incorrect tax returns. No detailed computations will be needed, especially on daily calculations of interest, but the principles will need to be understood.

Capital gains tax

Learners must appreciate who and what is taxable under this heading. The impact that relationships between connected persons have on disposal of capital assets needs to be understood.

Detailed computations can be expected on chargeable assets being disposed of, including enhancement expenditure and part disposals. Complications including shares are to be expected, including rights issues and bonus issues.

Explaining how capital assets will be taxed is just as important as the computational aspects. This is particularly relevant for some areas, such as principle private residences.

Tax returns

There are three areas where tax returns are assessable: employment income, property income and capital gains. These are expected to be completed with accuracy and completed in conjunction with the learners own figures.

TAX TABLES

Income tax rates and bands

	%	£
Savings income starting rate	10	first 2,440
Basic rate	20	first 37,400
Higher rate	40	over 37,400

Dividends are taxed at 10% and 32.5%.

Personal allowance: £6,475

Age allowance: £9,490 (ages 65 to 74)

£9,640 (age 75 +)

Car benefit percentage

The base level is 135g/km.

The base figure for fuel is £16,900.

10% for cars with CO_2 emissions of 120g/km or less.

HMRC official rate: 4.75%

Capital gains tax

Rate of tax	18%
Annual exempt amount	£10,100

chapter 1:
THE TAX FRAMEWORK

───────── **chapter coverage** 📖 ─────────

In this chapter we see that individuals pay income tax on their income, and capital gains tax on their chargeable gains, and that the rules governing these taxes are laid down in both Acts of Parliament and a body of law known as case law.

Finally, we consider the responsibilities that tax practitioners have to clients and Her Majesty's Revenue and Customs (HMRC), including client confidentiality.

The topics covered are:

✎ Tax position of individuals

✎ Relevant legislation and guidance from HMRC

✎ Responsibilities of tax practitioners

TAX POSITION OF INDIVIDUALS

Liability to tax

Individuals must pay income tax on their taxable income, and capital gains tax on any taxable gains arising on the disposal of chargeable assets. You will study income tax in the first part of this Text, and capital gains tax in the second part.

As a general rule, income is a receipt that is expected to recur (such as employment income), whereas a gain is a one-off profit on the disposal of a capital asset (eg the profit on the sale of a property held as an investment).

Her Majesty's Revenue and Customs

Income tax and capital gains tax are administered by HER MAJESTY'S REVENUE AND CUSTOMS (HMRC).

Tax year

Individuals must prepare personal tax computations for tax years. A TAX YEAR, FISCAL YEAR or YEAR OF ASSESSMENT is the year that runs from 6 April in one year to 5 April in the next. For example, the 2009/10 tax year runs from 6 April 2009 to 5 April 2010. Assessments from November 2009 will be based on the tax law that applies for the 2009/10 tax year until further notice from the AAT.

In some cases, HMRC send a taxpayer a tax return to be completed each tax year. However, most taxpayers have tax deducted from income before they receive it and this tax covers their tax liability so they are not sent a tax return by HMRC. We will look at tax returns in more detail when we consider the self-assessment system later in this Text.

Records

In order to complete a tax return or to show that the correct tax has been deducted at source, the taxpayer needs to have records of the income received, tax deducted and expenses incurred. Examples of such records include:

(a) Employment income: money earnings received (Form P60), taxable benefits (Form P11D), invoices for allowable expenses

(b) Property income: tenancy agreements, receipts for rent received and expenses paid

(c) Savings income: statements of interest received

(d) Dividend income: dividend certificates

(e) Capital gains: records of acquisition costs, enhancement costs, disposal costs, disposal proceeds

(f) General: details of gift aid donations made and statements of pension contributions to personal pension schemes

We look at records again when we consider the different types of income and how tax is calculated later in this Text.

Retention of records

HMRC may require taxpayers and third parties such as tax practitioners to produce records relating to a taxpayer's tax affairs.

Records must be retained until the later of:

(a) One year after the 31 January following the tax year concerned

(b) Five years after 31 January following the tax year concerned if the taxpayer carries on a business (trading income) or has property income, for example from renting out a house. In this case, the taxpayer must retain all records relating to the tax year, not just those dealing with the business or letting.

We look at the retention of records again when we consider the self-assessment system later in this Text.

HOW IT WORKS

Aleesha is employed by a firm of accountants. She also receives interest on her bank account.

She must retain records relating to income taxable in 2009/10 until 31 January 2012.

Task 1

Michael lets out a house in 2009/10 so has taxable property income for this year. He also receives some dividends from a company.

What is the date until which Michael must retain all his tax records for 2009/10?

31.01.2016

RELEVANT LEGISLATION AND GUIDANCE FROM HMRC

Statute law

Most of the rules governing income tax and capital gains tax are laid down in STATUTE LAW, which consists of Acts of Parliament. The existing Acts are amended each year in the annual Finance Act. This Text includes the provisions of the Finance Act 2009. This Act will be assessed from November 2010.

Some tax Acts provide for the making of detailed regulations by STATUTORY INSTRUMENT (SI). An example is the regulations which set out how employers deduct tax from employees' earnings under the Pay As You Earn (PAYE) system. A SI must be laid before Parliament and will usually become law automatically within a stated period unless any objections to it are raised.

Case law

Sometimes there may be a disagreement between HMRC and a taxpayer about how the tax legislation should be interpreted. In this situation either the taxpayer or HMRC may take the case to court. Cases about tax law are heard by the Tax Tribunal in the first instance.

Cases decided by the courts provide guidance on how legislation should be interpreted, and collectively form a second source of tax law known as CASE LAW.

You will not be expected to quote the names of decided cases in your assessment but you may need to know the principle decided in a case. Where relevant this will be noted within this Text.

HMRC guidance

To help taxpayers, HMRC publishes a wide range of guidance material on how it interprets tax law. These include:

(a)   Statements of practice, setting out how HMRC intend to apply the law

(b)   Extra-statutory concessions, setting out circumstances in which HMRC will not apply the strict letter of the law where it would be unfair

(c)   A wide range of explanatory leaflets

(d)   Revenue and Customs Briefs. These give HMRC's view on specific points

(e)   Internal Guidance, a series of manuals used by HMRC staff

(f)   Working Together, for tax practitioners

Much of this information can be found on HMRC's web site, www.hmrc.gov.uk. However, none of HMRC's guidance material has the force of law. Although you may like to have a look at this web site, you should find all you need for assessment purposes within this Text.

RESPONSIBILITIES OF TAX PRACTITIONERS

Responsibilities to clients and HMRC

Tax practitioners have a primary responsibility to act in the best interests of their clients. However, they also have a responsibility to deal with HMRC staff in an open and constructive manner which is consistent with the law.

AAT Guidelines on Professional Ethics

The AAT publish *Guidelines on Professional Ethics,* which set out a code of fundamental ethical principles and supporting guidance. These relate to the responsibilities that tax practitioners have to clients and to HMRC.

There are five fundamental principles which AAT members must follow:

(a) Integrity: a member must be straightforward and honest in all professional and business relationships

(b) Objectivity: a member must not allow bias, conflict of interest or undue influence of others to override professional or business judgements

(c) Professional competence and due care: a member has a continuing duty to maintain professional knowledge and skill at the level required to ensure that a client or employer receives competent professional service based on current developments in practice, legislation and techniques. A member must act diligently and in accordance with applicable technical and professional standards when providing professional services

(d) Confidentiality: see further below

(e) Professional behaviour: a member must comply with relevant laws and regulations and avoid conduct that brings the profession into disrepute

Confidentiality

The *Guidelines* state that an AAT member must, in accordance with the law, respect the confidentiality of information acquired as a result of professional and business relationships, and not disclose any such information to third parties without proper and specific authority unless there is a legal or professional right or duty to disclose. The *Guidelines* also state that confidential information acquired as a result of professional and business relationships must not be used for the personal advantage of the member or third parties.

HOW IT WORKS

You act for Sarah in relation to her tax affairs. You and Sarah have a mutual friend, Jeremy. Sarah knows that you act for Jeremy in relation to his tax affairs and Sarah asks you to tell her whether Jeremy has invested in an ISA as she is considering making a similar investment.

You must inform Sarah that, due to client confidentiality, you cannot discuss another client's affairs, even if they are friends. However, if Jeremy gives you specific authority to disclose information about his investments to Sarah, you may do so.

Task 2

Cornelius is an acquaintance of your client, Ruby, as they have similar jobs in similar sized companies. He knows that Ruby was made redundant recently. He is facing redundancy himself and would like to know how much redundancy money Ruby received so that he can compare this to the figure his company is offering him.

State how you should reply to this request for this information, clearly justifying your reply.

Disclosure of information to HMRC

There are circumstances where the law allows a breach of the duty of confidentiality. The main situation where this arises for a tax practitioner is the requirement to produce information to HMRC.

HMRC usually informally requests information and documents from taxpayers in connection with their tax affairs. If, however, a taxpayer does not co-operate fully, HMRC can request information and documents from a third party, such as a tax practitioner, by issuing a written 'information notice'. An information notice issued to a third party must be issued with the agreement of the taxpayer or the approval of the Tax Tribunal.

Tax practitioners cannot be asked to produce information connected with their function. For example, a tax practitioner does not have to produce access to working papers used in the preparation of the taxpayer's return. In addition, HMRC cannot ask a tax practitioner to produce communications between himself and either the taxpayer or his other advisers.

Material error or omission in client's tax return

The *Guidelines* state that when a member learns of a material error or omission in a tax return of a prior tax year or of a failure to file a required tax return, the member has a responsibility to advise the client of the error or omission and recommend that disclosure be made to HMRC. If the client, after having had a reasonable time to reflect, does not correct the error, the member should inform the client in writing that it is not possible for the member to act for them in connection with that return or other related information submitted to the authorities.

The *Guidelines* further state that a member in practice whose client refuses to make disclosure of an error or omission to HMRC, after having had notice of it and a reasonable time to reflect, is obliged to report the client's refusal and the facts surrounding it to the Money Laundering Reporting Officer (see below) within the firm, or to the appropriate authority (Serious Organised Crime Agency (SOCA) in the UK) if the member is a sole practitioner. The member must not disclose to the client or any one else that such a report has been made if the member knows or suspects that to do so would be likely to prejudice any investigation which might be conducted following the report.

We look at the penalties that may be imposed on a client who makes a material error or omission in his tax return when we consider the self-assessment system later in this Text.

Money laundering

MONEY LAUNDERING occurs when the proceeds of criminal activities are converted into assets that appear to have a non-criminal origin.

AAT members are bound by legislation to implement preventative measures and to report suspicions to the appropriate authority. Failure to follow these legislative requirements will often be a criminal offence, leading to a fine and/or imprisonment. Firms must have appropriate procedures to ensure that knowledge and suspicions of money laundering are reported to the firm's Money Laundering Reporting Officer. A sole practitioner should make a report directly to the appropriate authority such as SOCA.

CHAPTER OVERVIEW

- Individuals may have to pay income tax and/or capital gains tax
- HMRC is responsible for the administration of tax
- The tax year runs from 6 April in one year to the following 5 April
- Taxpayers must keep records of income received, tax deducted and expenses paid
- Taxpayers must keep records until the later of:
  - (a) One year after the 31 January following the tax year
  - (b) Five years after the 31 January following the tax year if in business or with property income
- Some of the rules governing tax are laid down in statute law, while some are laid down in case law
- HMRC provides guidance about how tax law works, for example in Statements of Practice, Extra Statutory Concessions and Revenue and Customs Briefs
- Tax practitioners have responsibilities to their clients and to HMRC
- The ethical *Guideline* of confidentiality means that a client's tax affairs should never be discussed with third parties without the client's permission
- Tax practitioners may be required to produce information to HMRC
- A tax practitioner must cease to act for a client who refuses to disclose an error or omission to HMRC, and must make a money laundering report
- Money laundering occurs when the proceeds of criminal activities are converted into assets which appear to have a non-criminal origin

Keywords

Her Majesty's Revenue and Customs (HMRC) – responsible for the administration of tax

The **Tax Year**, **Year of Assessment** or **Fiscal Year** – the year that runs from 6 April in one year to 5 April in the next year. Thus the tax year 2009/10 runs from 6 April 2009 to 5 April 2010

Statute law – legislation contained in Acts of Parliament

Statutory instrument – sets out detailed regulations relating to tax as authorised in a tax Act

Case law – decisions of the courts about the interpretation of tax statutes and is also a source of tax law

Money laundering – proceeds of criminal activities converted into assets which appear to have a non-criminal origin

TEST YOUR LEARNING

Test 1

True/False: All taxpayers are sent a tax return each year by Her Majesty's Revenue and Customs.

Test 2

Name the two sources of tax law.

Test 3

When is a tax practitioner not bound by the ethical *Guidelines* of client confidentiality?

A   When in a social environment

B   When discussing client affairs with third parties with the client's proper and specific authority

C   When reading documents relating to a client's affairs in public places

D   When preparing tax returns

Test 4

Who should a sole practitioner make a report to if he suspects a client of money laundering?

A   HMRC

B   Nearest police station

C   Serious Organised Crime Agency

D   Tax Tribunal

chapter 2:
EMPLOYMENT INCOME

chapter coverage 📖

In this chapter you start your studies of the calculation of employment income. We begin by considering how to decide whether an individual is employed or self-employed. We then learn about when earnings are received for tax purposes.

Next we see how to calculate the taxable value of employer-provided benefits, and consider what benefits are exempt from tax.

Then we look at some deductions that are allowable when computing taxable employment income.

We end the chapter by looking at the supplementary employment pages that must accompany an individual's income tax return form.

The topics covered are:

✍ Employment and self-employment

✍ Taxation of employment income

✍ Taxable benefits

✍ Exempt benefits

✍ Allowable deductions

✍ Employment tax pages

EMPLOYMENT AND SELF-EMPLOYMENT

It is important to be able to distinguish between employment (employment income) and self-employment (trading income). However, the distinction is a fine one. Employment is a contract of service, whereas self-employment is a contract for services.

It used to be thought that the deciding factor was the degree of control exercised by one party over the other about how the work should be done. The most that can be said now, however, is that control will always have to be considered, although it can no longer be regarded as the sole determining factor; other factors that may be of importance are such matters as:

(a) Whether the worker must be offered further work, and whether he must accept the work if offered (will indicate employment if this applies);

(b) Whether the person performing the services provides his own equipment (indicates self-employment);

(c) Whether he hires his own helpers (indicates self-employment);

(d) What degree of financial risk he takes (a high risk indicates self-employment);

(e) What degree of responsibility for investment and management he has (a high degree indicates self-employment); and

(f) Whether and how far he has an opportunity of profiting from sound management in the performance of his task (indicates self-employment);

(g) Whether he can work when he chooses (indicates self-employment);

(h) Whether he is entitled to holiday and sickness pay (indicates employment)

(i) The wording used in any agreement between the parties

In other words, the fundamental test to be applied is whether the person performing the services is performing them as a person in business on his own account. You may need to look at all of the above factors and form a view based on the balance of the evidence.

TAXATION OF EMPLOYMENT INCOME

Earnings from an office or employment are taxed as employment income.

Earnings include:

(a) Salaries, wages, bonuses, commissions, fees and tips ('money earnings')

(b) Any benefits provided by the employer ('taxable benefits' or 'benefits in kind')

(c)   Payments made on the termination of employment

We look at the first two types of earnings in this chapter, but the third type is not in your syllabus.

Certain allowable deductions can be made in the calculation of taxable earnings. We look at these later in this Chapter.

When are earnings received?

Earnings are taxed in the tax year in which they are received.

Money earnings are treated as received at the earlier of

(a)   The time when payment is made; and

(b)   The time when a person becomes entitled to payment of the earnings

HOW IT WORKS

Joy is employed by R plc. She is entitled to the payment of a bonus of £2,000 on 31 March 2010, although she does not receive it until 25 April 2010.

Joy will be taxed on the bonus in 2009/10 because she is entitled to payment on 31 March 2010.

Task 1

Rio is employed by BCD plc at an annual salary of £20,000. On 31 January 2010 he becomes entitled to and is paid a bonus of £5,000 relating to the company's profits for the year ended 31 December 2009.

Rio's earnings for 2009/10 are:

£   25,000

If the employee is a director of a company, his earnings from the company are received on the earliest of:

(a)   The time when payment is made; and

(b)   The time when a person becomes entitled to payment of the earnings

(c)   The time when the amount is credited in the company's accounting records

(d)   The end of the company's period of account (if the amount was determined by then)

(e)   The time the amount is determined (if after the end of the company's period of account)

HOW IT WORKS

Matt is a director of MN Ltd. On 25 March 2010, the company determines that it will pay Matt a bonus of £10,000 in relation to its period of account ending 31 March 2010. This is credited to Matt's director's account with the company on 10 April 2010 but he is not entitled to draw it until 30 April 2010. He actually draws out the payment from his account on 6 June 2010.

Matt is treated as receiving the bonus on 31 March 2010 (the end of the company's period of account) as the amount was determined by that time.

Task 2

Rita is a director of RS Ltd. On 10 April 2010, the company determines that it will pay Rita a bonus of £15,000 in relation to its period of account ending 31 December 2009. This is credited to Rita's director's account with the company on 15 June 2010 but she is not entitled to draw it until 31 July 2010. She actually draws out the payment on 31 October 2011.

Rita receives the bonus on:

A   31 December 2009
B   31 March 2010
C   10 April 2010
D   15 June 2010
E   31 July 2010
F   31 October 2011

Taxable benefits are generally received when they are provided to the employee.

Deduction of income tax by employer

An employer is required to deduct income tax from employees money earnings under the Pay As You Earn (PAYE) system. The employees therefore receive money earnings net of tax. The PAYE system also deals with taxable benefits. In most cases, this means that the employees have no further tax payable or repayable.

Details of the PAYE system are not in your syllabus.

TAXABLE BENEFITS

Taxable benefits are set out in legislation called the Benefits Code.

P11D employees

Most employees are known as P11D employees because their employer has to submit an annual P11D to HMRC in respect of the benefits provided to them.

Some very low paid employees are not P11D employees but the tax treatment of such individuals is not in your syllabus.

Company cars

If a car is provided for private use by reason of a person's employment a taxable benefit arises. This is sometimes called a "company car" benefit, although the rules apply whether the employer is a company or not. Private use includes home to work travel.

The benefit is normally a percentage of the car's list price. The maximum list price that can be used in calculating a taxable benefit is £80,000. The percentage for a car that emits between 121–135 grams of carbon dioxide per kilometre is 15%. This percentage increases by one percentage point for every additional 5 grams/kilometre (g/km) of CO_2 emissions, up to a maximum of 35%. The percentage is further increased by 3% for diesel cars (again up to the maximum of 35%). For cars which emit CO_2 of exactly 120g/km or less the percentage is 10%.

You will always be given a car's CO_2 emission rate in your assessment. If this is more than 135g/km, your first step in calculating a car benefit should be to round this down to the nearest 5g/km below the actual emissions. You then need to see by how many g/km the base figure of 135g/km is exceeded. We show how this works in the following example.

HOW IT WORKS

Nigel is provided with a petrol engined car which had a list price of £22,000. The car has CO_2 emissions of 198g/km.

Nigel's taxable car benefit for 2009/10 is calculated as follows:

First, round down 198 g/km to 195 g/km.

Then calculate the amount by which the base figure is exceeded, in this case 60g/km (195 – 135).

Then increase the taxable percentage by 1% for every 5g/km above the base figure, ie increase it by 60/5 = 12%.

The taxable percentage is 15% + 12%   = 27%

So the car benefit is £22,000 × 27%   = £5,940

If an employee makes a capital contribution towards the cost of a car, the contribution is deducted from the list price used for calculating the benefit, subject to a maximum deduction of £5,000. If, however, an employee makes a payment for the private use of a car (as distinct from a capital contribution to the cost of the car), the payment is deducted in calculating the taxable benefit.

The car benefit is pro-rated if the car is only provided for part of the year or if it is incapable of being used for 30 or more consecutive days.

HOW IT WORKS

Vicky starts her employment on 6 January 2010 and is immediately provided with a new petrol engine car with a list price of £25,000. The car was more expensive than her employer would have provided and she therefore made a capital contribution of £6,200. Vicky contributes £100 a month for being able to use the car privately. CO_2 emissions are 262g/km. Vicky's car benefit for 2009/10 is:

	£
List price	25,000
Less: capital contributions (maximum)	(5,000)
	20,000

£20,000 × 35% (W) = £7,000

	£
3/12 × £7,000	1,750
Less: contribution to running costs (£100 × 3)	(300)
Car benefit	1,450

Working

CO_2 emissions = 260 g/km (rounded down).

The amount by which the base figure is exceeded is 125 g/km (260 – 135).

125/5 = 25

Taxable percentage = 15% + 25% = 40% but restrict to 35% maximum.

The taxable car benefit covers all expenditure by the employer on repairs, servicing, insurance, road fund licence and cleaning of the car. No additional benefit arises in respect of these items. A taxable benefit does, however, arise in respect of a chauffeur provided for private mileage. This will be based on the cost of the chauffeur.

Task 3

On 6 July 2009 Sue was provided with a new petrol driven car by her employer. The list price of the car was £10,000. The car's CO_2 emissions are 218g/km. The taxable benefit on the provision of the car is:

£ [   ]

Fuel provided for private use

If an employer pays for fuel used for private motoring in a company car, a fuel benefit arises.

The benefit is a percentage of a base figure. The base figure for 2009/10 is £16,900. The percentage is the same percentage as is used to calculate the car benefit.

No benefit arises where it can be shown that either all the fuel provided was used only for business travel or that the employee has reimbursed the whole of the expense of any fuel provided for his private use.

There is **no** reduction to the benefit if only part of the expense for private use fuel is reimbursed by the employee.

The fuel benefit is reduced if private fuel is not available for part of a tax year. However, if private fuel later becomes available in the same tax year, there is no reduction made.

HOW IT WORKS

An employee was provided with a new petrol engine car costing £15,000 (the list price) on 6 June 2009. During 2009/10 the employer spent £900 on insurance, repairs and the vehicle licence. The firm paid for all petrol (£2,300) without reimbursement. The employee was required to pay the firm £25 per month for the private use of the car. The car has CO_2 emissions of 135g/km.

The total taxable benefit for 2009/10 in respect of the car and fuel is calculated as follows:

Car was available for ten months.

	£
List price £15,000 × 15%	2,250
£2,250 × 10/12	1,875
Less: contribution (10 × £25)	(250)
	1,625
Fuel benefit £16,900 × 15% × 10/12	2,112
Taxable benefit	3,737

If the contribution of £25 per month had been towards the petrol, the benefit assessable would have been £(1,875 + 2,112) = £3,987. Conversely, if the cost of private petrol were fully reimbursed by the employee then there would have been no fuel benefit at all.

Task 4

Nissar had the use of a company car throughout 2009/10. The list price of the car was £30,000. The car had a diesel engine and CO_2 emissions of 194g/km. The company provided fuel for both private and business motoring. Nissar made a contribution of £400 towards the cost of private fuel.

The total taxable benefit arising to Nissar in 2009/10 is:

A   £7,800
B   £13,976
C   £12,194
D   £13,601

Pool cars

The private use of a pool car is an exempt benefit. A car is a pool car if all the following conditions are satisfied:

(a)   It is used by more than one employee and is not ordinarily used by any one of them to the exclusion of the others

(b)   Any private use is merely incidental to business use

(c)   It is not normally kept overnight at or near the residence of an employee

Vans provided for private use

Where a van is provided to an employee that is available for private use, there is an annual scale charge of £3,000. There is not a taxable benefit if there is no private use allowed. Private use does not include home to work travel (compare to cars where home to work travel is private use). There is an additional fuel benefit of £500 if fuel is provided for private use.

Assets made available for private use

In general, if an employee uses an employer-owned asset privately, an annual benefit arises equal to 20% of the market value of the asset when first used by the employee.

If the asset is subsequently acquired by the employee, the benefit arising on the acquisition is usually the greater of:

(a)   The market value of the asset on acquisition; and

(b) The market value of the asset when first provided to the employee less any amounts already assessed as a benefit.

HOW IT WORKS

A suit costing £200 is bought by an employer for use by an employee on 6 April 2008. On 6 April 2009 the suit is purchased by the employee for £15, its market value then being £25.

The taxable benefit in 2009/10 is calculated as follows:

The benefit taxable in 2008/09 will be 20% × £200 = £40

The benefit taxable in 2009/10 will be the greater of:

(a) Market value at acquisition by employee = £25

(b)

	£	£
Original market value	200	
Less: assessed in respect of use 2008/09	(40)	
	160	
ie		160
Less: price paid by employee		(15)
Taxable benefit 2009/10		145

Task 5

Ahmed bought video equipment from his employer on 6 July 2009 for £1,000. The equipment was then worth £4,000. Ahmed had first used the equipment on 6 April 2008 when his employer had lent it to him for private use. The market value of the equipment was £6,000 on 6 April 2008.

The taxable benefit for use arising in 2008/09 is:

£ 1200

and in 2009/10 is:

£ 300

and the taxable benefit on Ahmed's acquisition in 2009/10 is:

£ 3500

Beneficial loans

Employer loans give rise to a benefit equal to:

(a) Any amounts written-off; and

(b) The excess of the official rate of interest on the loan over any interest actually charged.

There are two methods of calculating the interest benefit. The 'average' method applies automatically unless an election is made by the taxpayer or HMRC. (HMRC normally only make the election where it appears that the 'average' method is being deliberately exploited.)

The first method averages the balance of the loan at the beginning and end of the tax year (or the dates on which the loan was made and discharged if it was not in existence throughout the year) and applies the official rate of interest to this average. If the loan was not in existence throughout the year, only the number of complete tax months (from the sixth of the month) for which it existed are taken into account.

The second method is to compute interest at the official rate on a daily basis on the actual amount outstanding.

HOW IT WORKS

At 6 April 2009 a low interest loan of £30,000 was outstanding to a director, who repaid £20,000 on 6 December 2009. The remaining balance of £10,000 was outstanding at 5 April 2010. Interest paid during the year was £250.

The benefit under both methods for 2009/10, assuming that the official rate of interest was 4.75% throughout 2009/10, is calculated as follows:

Average method

	£
$4.75\% \times \dfrac{(30,000 + 10,000)}{2}$	950
Less: interest paid	(250)
Taxable benefit	700

Alternative method

	£
£30,000 × 8/12	
(6 April 2009 – 5 December 2009) × 4.75%	950
£10,000 × 4/12	
(6 December 2009 – 5 April 2010) × 4.75%	158
	1,108
Less: interest paid	(250)
Taxable benefit	858

No taxable benefit arises if the total balance on all loans to the employee did not exceed £5,000 at any time in the year.

When the £5,000 threshold is exceeded, a benefit arises on interest on the whole loan, not just on the excess of the loan over £5,000.

When a loan is written-off and a benefit arises, there is no £5,000 threshold: writing-off a loan of £1 gives rise to a £1 benefit.

HOW IT WORKS

Annika has two loans from her employer:

(a) A season ticket loan of £2,300 at no interest

(b) A loan of £24,000 at 2% interest which Annika used to buy a holiday cottage

The official rate of interest is 4.75%.

As the total of the loans exceeds £5,000 a taxable benefit arises in respect of both loans.

The taxable benefit that arises in respect of the loans in 2009/10 is calculated as follows:

	£
£2,300 × 4.75%	109
£24,000 × (4.75% − 2%)	660
	769

Task 6

On 6 April 2009 Anton's employer provided him with an interest-free season ticket loan of £6,200. He repaid £1,000 of this loan on 6 October 2009. The official rate of interest is 4.75%. The taxable benefit arising in respect of the loan assuming no elections are made is:

£ 271

Task 7

An employer lends an employee £4,000 to buy a car, interest-free for six months. The official rate of interest is 4.75%. 65% of the loan is then repaid, and the balance is written-off. The total taxable benefit?

£ 1400

Accommodation

If an employer provides an employee with accommodation, there is a basic benefit equal to the higher of:

(a) The 'annual value' of the property (given in the assessment); and

(b) Any rent actually paid for the property by the employer (if the property is rented rather than owned by the employer).

The benefit is reduced by any contribution the employee makes for the use of the property.

The benefit is exempt if the accommodation is job-related (see further below).

HOW IT WORKS

Tony is provided with a company flat:

	£
Annual value	300
Rent paid by the company	3,380
Amount paid by Tony to the company for the use of the flat	520

Tony's taxable benefit is:

	£
Benefit: greater of:	
(a) annual value	£300
(b) rent paid	£3,380
ie	3,380
Less: reimbursed to the company	(520)
Net benefit	2,860

If the cost of employer-provided accommodation exceeds £75,000, an additional benefit arises. The amount of the additional benefit is equal to:

ORI × (C − £75,000)

ORI is the official rate of interest at the start of the tax year. This will be given to you in the assessment.

C is the cost of providing the accommodation. This includes the cost of purchase and the cost of any improvements made before the start of the tax year.

If the accommodation was acquired by the employer more than six years before it was first provided to the employee, and its original cost plus improvements exceeded £75,000, the 'cost of providing' is increased to its market value when first provided to that employee.

Where any contribution paid by the employee exceeds the annual value of the property, the excess may be deducted from the additional benefit.

HOW IT WORKS

Simon's employer provided him with a house throughout 2009/10. The company bought the house for £133,000 on 1 April 2005.

For 2009/10, the annual value of the house is £1,400. Simon pays £3,000 for the use of the house to his employer.

The total benefit for 2009/10 arising in respect of the house, assuming the official rate of interest is 4.75% is:

Basic charge:

		£
Annual value		1,400
Less: contribution		(1,400)
		NIL

Additional charge:

	£	£
Cost	133,000	
Less:		(75,000)
Excess	58,000	
£58,000 × 4.75%		2,755
Less: contribution (£3,000 – 1,400)		(1,600)
Total benefit 2009/10		1,155

Task 8

Throughout 2009/10 Marak lived in a house provided by his employer. The following information is relevant:

Annual value	£5,200
Cost of the house (bought by employer in 2008)	£600,000
Rent paid by Marak in 2009/10	£12,000
Official rate of interest throughout 2009/10	4.75%

> The taxable value of the accommodation provided in 2009/10 is:
>
> A   £18,138
> B   £12,938
> C   £30,138
> D   £21,700

Expenses connected with living accommodation

The following living expenses incurred in connection with living accommodation give rise to a taxable benefit:

(a)   Heating, lighting or cleaning the premises

(b)   Repairing, maintaining or decorating them

(c)   Providing furniture etc normal for domestic occupation (annual value taken as 20% of cost)

If the accommodation is job-related no accommodation benefit is chargeable (see below). The maximum chargeable benefit in respect of the above expenses is 10% of the employee's net earnings, ie salary plus all other taxable benefits less any allowable deductions.

Task 9

Mr Quinton has a gross salary in 2009/10 of £27,400. He is required to live in job-related accommodation. The annual value of the house is £650. In 2009/10 the company pays an electricity bill of £550, a gas bill of £400, a gardener's bill of £750 and redecoration costs of £1,800. Mr Quinton makes a monthly contribution of £50 for his accommodation. The accommodation qualifies as job-related.

Calculate Mr Quinton's taxable employment income for 2009/10.

Vouchers

An employee is normally taxable on the cost to the employer of providing a voucher or credit token (eg a credit card).

However, if the employee receives a cash voucher, he will be taxable on the amount for which the voucher can be exchanged.

Certain vouchers are exempt. These are included in the list of exempt benefits later in this chapter.

Statutory mileage rate scheme

Where employers pay mileage allowances to employees who use their own vehicles for business travel, the employees are taxed on any amounts received in excess of the STATUTORY MILEAGE RATE SCHEME rates. The mileage rates for cars are 40p a mile for the first 10,000 miles and 25p a mile thereafter. There are separate mileage rates for motorcycles and bicycles. If you need any of these rates, they will be given to you in the assessment.

If there is no allowance, or if the allowance received by the employee is less than the amount calculated using the statutory rates, the employee may deduct the shortfall when calculating taxable earnings.

HOW IT WORKS

Owen drives 14,000 business miles in 2009/10 using his own car.

You are required to calculate the taxable benefit/allowable deduction assuming:

    (a)   He is reimbursed 40p a mile
    (b)   He is reimbursed 25p a mile

		£
Statutory limit:	10,000 × 40p	4,000
	4,000 × 25p	1,000
		5,000

(a)		£
	Amount received (14,000 × 40p)	5,600
	Less: statutory limit	(5,000)
	Taxable benefit	600

(b)		£
	Amount received (14,000 × 25p)	3,500
	Less: statutory limit	(5,000)
	Allowable deduction	(1,500)

Task 10

Yarrik used his car to travel 12,000 business miles in 2009/10. His employer paid him 38p per business mile travelled. The taxable benefit arising on Yarrik in respect of the amount paid to him by his employer is:

£ _____

Task 11

Megan uses her own car for business travel and her employer reimburses her 25p per mile. In 2009/10 Megan drove 12,000 business miles. What is Megan's tax position in respect of the business mileage?

EXEMPT BENEFITS

There is a fairly long list of benefits that are not taxable on employees, including:

(a) **Accommodation**

Living accommodation that constitutes JOB-RELATED ACCOMMODATION. Accommodation is job-related if:

(i) Residence in the accommodation is necessary for the proper performance of the employee's duties (eg a caretaker); or

(ii) Accommodation is provided for the better performance of the employee's duties and the employment is of a kind in which it is customary for accommodation to be provided (eg a vicar or policeman); or

(iii) The accommodation is provided as part of special security arrangements in force because of a special threat to the employee's security (eg the Prime Minister).

(b) **Subsistence**

(i) Meals in a staff canteen, if they are available to all employees on broadly similar terms.

(ii) The first 15p per working day of meal vouchers.

(iii) Personal incidental expenses of up to £5 per night for employees working away from home in the UK, or £10 per night if working abroad that would otherwise be taxable (eg laundry, newspapers, telephone calls home).

However, where more than one night is spent away, the exemption works on an aggregate basis, eg for four nights the overall limit is £20.

(c) **Travel**

(i) Use of a pool car (see above).

(ii) The provision of a parking space at or near the place of work.

(iii) Mileage allowances for cars, motor bikes and bicycles within the statutory limits (see above).

(iv) The provision of works buses with a seating capacity of nine or more that are used mainly to bring employees to and from work.

    (v)   The payment of general subsidies to public bus services used by employees to travel to work.

    (vi) The provision of bicycles and cycling safety equipment made available for employees mainly to travel between home and work.

    (vii) Tax-free breakfasts on official 'cycle to work' days.

(d) **Removal expenses**: up to £8,000 of removal expenses borne by the employer where the employee has to move house on first taking up the employment or on a transfer within the organisation.

(e) **Entertainment**: the provision of staff parties provided that the cost is no more than £150 per head per annum.

(f) **Childcare**: the cost of running a workplace nursery or play scheme (without limit). Otherwise up to £55 a week is tax-free if the employer contracts with an approved child carer or provides childcare vouchers to pay an approved child carer. The childcare must be available to all employees and the childcare must be registered or approved home child-care.

(g) **Home-working**: a tax-free allowance of up to £3 per week is payable to employees to cover the additional household costs of working some or all of the time at home. No record keeping is required for the flat-rate allowance. For payments above that figure, evidence will be required that the payment is wholly in respect of additional household expenses incurred by the employee in carrying out their duties at home.

(h) **Work-related training and related costs**: this includes the costs of training material and assets either made during training or incorporated into something so made.

(i) **Payments by the employer to registered pension schemes**: to provide pension benefits for employees (see later in this Chapter).

(j) **Miscellaneous**

    (i)   Non-cash long service awards – for service in excess of 20 years, £50 per year of service is tax-free.

    (ii) Awards under a formally constituted staff suggestion scheme open to all employees on equal terms, for a suggestion outside the scope of the employee's normal duties. The award must either be not more than £25 or made after a decision is made to implement the suggestion. Awards over £25 must reflect the financial importance of the suggestion to the business and must either not exceed 50% of the expected net financial benefit during the first year of implementation or not exceed 10% of the expected net financial benefit over a period of up to five years. Awards of over £25 must be shared on a reasonable basis between two or more employees putting forward the same suggestion. If an award exceeds £5,000, the excess over £5,000 is always taxable.

(iii) Workplace sports or recreational facilities provided by employers for use by their staff generally. This does not apply where the employer pays or reimburses an employee's subscription to a sports club, nor where the facilities are only available to limited groups of employees.

(iv) Air miles obtained in the course of business travel.

(v) The private use of one mobile phone by the employee. If more than one mobile phone is provided to an employee for his private use or a phone is provided to a member of the employee's family, a taxable benefit arises based on the cost to the employer of provision of these phones.

ALLOWABLE DEDUCTIONS

The following expenditure can be deducted in the calculation of taxable earnings:

(a) Contributions to a registered occupational pension scheme

(b) Subscriptions to professional bodies, if relevant to the duties of employment

(c) Donations to charity under an approved payroll deduction scheme

(d) Qualifying travel expenses

(e) Other expenses incurred wholly, exclusively and necessarily in the performance of the duties of employment

We now look at these deductions in more detail.

Contributing to a pension

An individual may make pension provision in a number of ways.

If the individual is employed, he may join an occupational pension scheme run by his employer that is registered with HMRC.

Any individual (whether employed or not) may join a personal pension scheme run by a financial institution such as an insurance company or a bank.

An individual may make a number of different pension arrangements depending on his circumstances. For example, he may be a member of an occupational pension scheme and also make pension arrangements independently with a financial provider. If the individual has more than one pension arrangement, the rules noted below apply to all the pension arrangements he makes. For example, there is a limit on the amount of contributions that an individual can make in a tax year. This limit applies to all the pension arrangements that he makes, not *each* of them.

Each tax year an individual under the age of 75 may make tax-relievable pension contributions of up to the higher of:

(a) His earnings

(b) The basic amount (£3,600 in 2009/10)

Individuals with no earnings can, therefore, contribute £3,600 to a pension scheme each year.

Tax relief for contributions to occupational pension schemes is usually given under NET PAY ARRANGEMENTS. This means the employer deducts the contributions from the employee's earnings before he deducts income tax under the PAYE system.

An employer may also make contributions to a pension scheme as part of an employment benefits package. Such contributions are exempt benefits for the employee. Sometimes the employer may run a non-contributory occupational pension scheme, which means that only the employer makes contributions to the scheme but not the employee. However, such pension schemes are now relatively rare.

Contributions to schemes run by personal pension providers are given tax relief in a different way. We look at this method of giving tax relief when we deal with the calculation of income tax later in this Text.

Payments from occupational pension schemes to pensioners are made after deduction of income tax under the PAYE system.

Charitable donations under payroll deduction scheme

If an employer has set up a PAYROLL DEDUCTION SCHEME , employees can make tax-deductible donations to an approved charity of their choice by asking the employer to deduct a donation from their gross earnings before deducting income tax under the PAYE system. This method of making tax deductible donations to charity is sometimes called "Give As You Earn" or GAYE.

Qualifying travel expenses

Travel expenses are deductible if they are either incurred:

(a) On business travel, or

(b) On travelling to a TEMPORARY WORKPLACE. A workplace is temporary if the employee will return to his normal workplace at the end of a temporary period and the temporary period lasts for less than 24 months.

Travel from home to work is not allowable.

Statutory mileage rate scheme

If an employee uses his own vehicle for business travel, the cost (to the extent that it is not reimbursed) can be claimed as a deduction, under the statutory mileage rate scheme (see above).

Expenses incurred wholly, exclusively and necessarily in the performance of the duties of an employment

Expenses incurred wholly, exclusively and necessarily in the performance of the duties of an employment are allowable deductions when calculating employment income.

Examples include travelling for business purposes, entertaining customers and subsistence costs such as meals and hotel expenses.

The test of deductibility is applied quite strictly. For example, none of the cost of renting a phone line is deductible if the phone is also used for private purposes. This is because the line is not used 'exclusively' for business purposes.

Strictly, any other expenses that have a private element are not deductible but, in practice, taxpayers are usually allowed to apportion expenses between parts that are for private purposes and those that are for business purposes. The business part of an expense is deductible.

Reimbursement of expenditure

Sometimes an employee may incur expenditure that is then reimbursed by the employer, such as business entertaining expenditure or costs of business travel, including staying in hotels. The payment by the employer will be a benefit under the Benefits Code, but the expenditure by the employee may also be an allowable deduction under the rules we have just looked at.

There are two possible treatments of the reimbursement:

(a) The employer may have agreed a dispensation with HMRC that the reimbursement and the expenditure by the employee will be ignored for tax purposes.

(b) In his employment pages, the employee should include the payment by the employer as a taxable benefit but also enter his expenditure as an allowable deduction. The two entries will cancel each other out to the extent that the expenditure is allowable.

EMPLOYMENT TAX PAGES

In your assessment you may have to complete the supplementary employment pages that accompany the income tax return form. We have included a sample of these pages at the end of this chapter. Have a look at them now. You will be able to practise using this form in the Personal Tax Question Bank.

CHAPTER OVERVIEW

- It is important to distinguish between income from an employment (assessable as employment income) and self-employment (assessable as trading income). The basic question is whether the person is employed under a contract of service, or performs services under a contract for services and is therefore self-employed

- An employee's earnings comprise not only his wages or salary but also employer-provided benefits

- Money earnings are generally received on the earlier of the time payment is made and when the employee becomes entitled to payment. There are special rules for directors

- The taxable benefit arising on a car provided for private use is a percentage of the car's list price. This percentage is 15% for cars that emit between 121–135g/km of CO_2, 10% for cars emitting CO_2 of exactly 120g/km or less, and for cars emitting more than 135g/km the % increases by 1% for each additional 5g/km up to 35%

- The private use of a pool car is an exempt benefit

- There is a taxable benefit of £3,000 a year for private use of a van (but home to work travel is not treated as private use) plus £500 if private fuel is provided

- If the employer provides the employee with assets for private use, there is a taxable benefit each year of 20% of the value of the assets when first provided

- Employer loans written-off give rise to a taxable benefit equal to the loan written-off. For a loan outstanding during the year, there is a taxable benefit equal to the excess of the official rate of interest on the loan over any interest actually charged

- The living accommodation benefit is based on the annual value of the property. An additional benefit arises where the cost of the property, or in certain circumstances the market value at the date it is first occupied, exceeds £75,000

- A deduction from taxable earnings is given to employees for the cost of using their own vehicle for business travel if any mileage allowance paid is less than the statutory rates. Any excess is taxable

- Expenses incurred by the employer in connection with the provision of living accommodation are fully assessable on the employee/director, unless the employee/ director is in job-related accommodation. In the latter case, the maximum benefit is 10% of the net earnings from the employment

- There are certain exempt benefits which are not taxable on employees (eg the provision of meals in a staff canteen)

- Occupational pension schemes are employer run schemes. No taxable benefit arises in respect of employer contributions made to such schemes

- Contributions to an occupational pension scheme are usually deducted from the employee's taxable earnings

- Individuals can make pension contributions up to the higher of:
  (a)   The basic limit (£3,600 – 2009/10)
  (b)   Earnings

- Employees can make charitable donations under an employer's payroll deduction scheme. Such payments are deductible in arriving at taxable earnings

- Employees are generally allowed a deduction for travel costs incurred in the performance of their duties or incurred in travelling to and from a temporary workplace. Temporary is taken to be not exceeding 24 months

- For other employment-related expenses to be deductible, such expenses must be 'wholly, exclusively and necessarily' incurred 'in the performance of' the employee's duties

Keywords

The statutory mileage rate scheme – lays down authorised rates at which employees may claim an allowance for business journeys made in their own car

A temporary workplace – one at which the employee expects to be for less than 24 months

Job-related accommodation – accommodation that is either necessary for the proper performance of duties, is customarily provided, or is provided as part of special security arrangements

Net pay arrangements – where an employer deducts pension contributions from an employee's earnings before he deducts income tax

A payroll deduction scheme – set up by an employer to enable employees to make tax-deductible donations to charity

TEST YOUR LEARNING

Test 1

Someone is regarded as self-employed if he has a contract ...., whereas if he has a contract ...., he will be regarded as an employee.

Fill in the missing words.

Test 2

Expenses are deductible in computing taxable earnings if they are incurred ...., ... and .... in the performance of the duties of employment.

Fill in the missing words.

Test 3

Brian uses his own car to travel 8,000 business miles in 2009/10. Brian's employer reimburses him with 35p per mile travelled. The statutory mileage rate for the first 10,000 business miles travelled is 40p per mile.

The amounts that are taxable/(deductible) in calculating employment income are:

£

Test 4

An employee is provided with a flat by his employer (not job-related accommodation). The annual value of the flat is £400; rent paid by the employer amounts to £3,900 per annum.

The taxable value of this benefit is:

£

Test 5

True/False: a taxable fuel benefit is reduced by any reimbursement by the employee of the cost of fuel provided for private mileage.

Test 6

A video recorder costing £500 was made available to Gordon by his employer on 6 April 2008. On 6 April 2009, Gordon bought the recorder for £150, when its market value was £325. The assessable benefit that arises in 2009/10 is:

A   £325

B   £400

C   £175

D   £250

Test 7

True/False: the first £5,000 of an interest-free loan is exempt from tax.

Test 8

Gautown was supplied with a petrol engined car by his employer throughout 2009/10. The list price of the car was £24,000 and its CO_2 emissions are 182 g/km. The taxable benefit arising in respect of the car is:

£

Test 9

Buster is the Managing Director of Buster Braces Ltd and is supplied with a Bentley (three litre, petrol engine) which cost £72,000. It has CO_2 emissions of 195g/km. All running costs are borne by the company. Buster is also provided with a mobile phone for private business use. The cost of provision of the phone to Buster Braces Ltd is £750 in 2009/10. What are the total taxable benefits?

Employment

Tax year 6 April 2009 to 5 April 2010

Your name	Your unique taxpayer reference (UTR)

Complete an *Employment* page for each employment or directorship

1 Pay from this employment – the total from your P45 or P60 – *before tax was taken off*

£ . 0 0

2 UK tax taken off pay in box 1

£ . 0 0

3 Tips and other payments not on your P60 – *read page EN 3 of the notes*

£ . 0 0

4 PAYE tax reference of your employer (on your P45/P60)

/

5 Your employer's name

6 If you were a company director, put 'X' in the box

7 And, if the company was a close company, put 'X' in the box

8 If you are a part-time teacher in England or Wales and are on the Repayment of Teachers' Loans Scheme for this employment, put 'X' in the box

Benefits from your employment – use your form P11D (or equivalent information)

9 Company cars and vans – *the total 'cash equivalent' amount*

£ . 0 0

10 Fuel for company cars and vans – *the total 'cash equivalent' amount*

£ . 0 0

11 Private medical and dental insurance – *the total 'cash equivalent' amount*

£ . 0 0

12 Vouchers, credit cards and excess mileage allowance

£ . 0 0

13 Goods and other assets provided by your employer – *the total value or amount*

£ . 0 0

14 Accommodation provided by your employer – *the total value or amount*

£ . 0 0

15 Other benefits (including interest-free and low interest loans) – *the total 'cash equivalent' amount*

£ . 0 0

16 Expenses payments received and balancing charges

£ . 0 0

Employment expenses

17 Business travel and subsistence expenses

£ . 0 0

18 Fixed deductions for expenses

£ . 0 0

19 Professional fees and subscriptions

£ . 0 0

20 Other expenses and capital allowances

£ . 0 0

Shares schemes, employment lump sums, compensation, deductions and Seafarers' Earnings Deduction are on the *Additional information* pages enclosed in the tax return pack

SA102 2010   Tax return: Employment: Page E 1   HMRC 12/09 net ℹ️ Shares schemes, employment lump sums, compensation, deductions and Seafarers' Earnings Deduction are on the *Additional information* pages enclosed in the tax return pack

Second employment

Complete an *Employment* page for each employment or directorship

1 Pay from this employment - the total from your P45 or P60 - *before tax was taken off*

£ ⬜⬜⬜⬜⬜⬜⬜⬜ · 0 0

5 Your employer's name

⬜

2 UK tax taken off pay in box 1

£ ⬜⬜⬜⬜⬜⬜⬜⬜ · 0 0

6 If you were a company director, put 'X' in the box

⬜

3 Tips and other payments not on your P60 - *read page EN 3 of the notes*

£ ⬜⬜⬜⬜⬜⬜⬜⬜ · 0 0

7 And, if the company was a close company, put 'X' in the box

⬜

4 PAYE tax reference of your employer (on your P45/P60)

⬜⬜⬜ / ⬜⬜⬜⬜⬜⬜⬜⬜⬜⬜

8 If you are a part-time teacher in England or Wales and are on the Repayment of Teachers' Loans Scheme for this employment, put 'X' in the box

⬜

Benefits from your employment - use your form P11D (or equivalent information)

9 Company cars and vans - *the total 'cash equivalent' amount*

£ ⬜⬜⬜⬜⬜⬜⬜⬜ · 0 0

13 Goods and other assets provided by your employer - *the total value or amount*

£ ⬜⬜⬜⬜⬜⬜⬜⬜ · 0 0

10 Fuel for company cars and vans - *the total 'cash equivalent' amount*

£ ⬜⬜⬜⬜⬜⬜⬜⬜ · 0 0

14 Accommodation provided by your employer - *the total value or amount*

£ ⬜⬜⬜⬜⬜⬜⬜⬜ · 0 0

11 Private medical and dental insurance - *the total 'cash equivalent' amount*

£ ⬜⬜⬜⬜⬜⬜⬜⬜ · 0 0

15 Other benefits (including interest-free and low interest loans) - *the total 'cash equivalent' amount*

£ ⬜⬜⬜⬜⬜⬜⬜⬜ · 0 0

12 Vouchers, credit cards and excess mileage allowance

£ ⬜⬜⬜⬜⬜⬜⬜⬜ · 0 0

16 Expenses payments received and balancing charges

£ ⬜⬜⬜⬜⬜⬜⬜⬜ · 0 0

Employment expenses

17 Business travel and subsistence expenses

£ ⬜⬜⬜⬜⬜⬜⬜⬜ · 0 0

19 Professional fees and subscriptions

£ ⬜⬜⬜⬜⬜⬜⬜⬜ · 0 0

18 Fixed deductions for expenses

£ ⬜⬜⬜⬜⬜⬜⬜⬜ · 0 0

20 Other expenses and capital allowances

£ ⬜⬜⬜⬜⬜⬜⬜⬜ · 0 0

chapter 3:
PROPERTY INCOME

chapter coverage 📖

In this chapter we first see what property income is and then how to compute the property income that a landlord is taxed on in a tax year. We also look at how losses on lettings are given tax relief.

We then look at the special rules that apply for qualifying holiday accommodation and renting rooms in the taxpayer's main residence (rent-a-room relief).

We end the chapter by looking at the supplementary land and property pages that must accompany the income tax return form of an individual who has let property in the tax year concerned.

The topics covered are:

✍ What is property income?

✍ Computing property income

✍ Losses

✍ Qualifying holiday accommodation

✍ Rent-a-room relief

✍ Land and Property tax form pages

WHAT IS PROPERTY INCOME?

Property income is income that arises from letting out land and buildings. It can include rental income from letting out a piece of land (for example a field for grazing animals), a building such as a house, or part of a building such as a shop or a flat. The person who lets out the land or buildings is called the LANDLORD. The person who occupies the land or buildings is called the TENANT.

In the case of letting out a property in which the tenant lives, the landlord may provide furniture for the tenant to use. This is called a FURNISHED LETTING. If the tenant provides the furniture, the landlord's letting is called an UNFURNISHED LETTING. As you will see later in this chapter there are some different tax rules for furnished and unfurnished lettings.

Sometimes a taxpayer may buy a property specifically with the intention of letting it out and, possibly, benefitting from an increase in its capital value in the future. This may be called a BUY-TO-LET INVESTMENT. The same rules apply to buy-to-let investments as for any other property letting.

COMPUTING PROPERTY INCOME

Property income is taxed as non-savings income on an ACCRUALS BASIS. The accruals basis means that all rental income accruing in a tax year is taxed in that year. The date that the income is actually received by the landlord is not relevant.

HOW IT WORKS

Susi bought a property on 6 September 2009. Susi began letting the property immediately for an annual rent of £36,000 payable in advance in three-monthly instalments due on 6 September, 6 December, 6 March and 6 June.

Rental income is taxed on an accruals basis. This means the income which arises from the letting for the period between 6 September 2009 and 5 April 2010 is taxed in 2009/10. Susi is therefore taxed on £36,000 × 7/12 = £21,000. She actually receives instalments of £9,000 on 6 September, 6 December and 6 March in the tax year, giving total receipts of £27,000, but this is not relevant for the tax calculation.

Expenses are also allowed on an accruals basis if they are revenue expenses (rather than capital expenses) that are wholly and exclusively incurred for the purpose of letting. Common allowable expenses include:

(a) Advertising for tenants, accountancy and insurance

(b) Business and water rates and council tax

(c) Bad debts if a rent payment appears unlikely to be recoverable, for example if the tenant has left the property and cannot be traced

(d) Management and agents fees

(e) Maintenance and repair costs such as redecoration

(f) Loan interest and overdraft interest if the related borrowing was applied wholly and exclusively for the purposes of letting the property

Common expenses which are not allowable include:

(a) Expenses relating to the landlord's own use of the property

(b) Capital expenses such as replacing central heating, construction of walls and extensions, replacement (rather than repair) of roofs, fitted kitchens and bathrooms

HOW IT WORKS

Nadine has let a property unfurnished for many years. She charged rental income of £40,000 for the year to 31 December 2009. The annual rent rose to £44,000 with effect from 1 January 2010.

Expenses relating to the letting were:

	£
Water rates (year to 31 March 2010)	2,000
Insurance (year to 31 December 2009)	600
Insurance (year to 31 December 2010)	800
Agents fees – 10% of rental income	

In June 2009 the tenant accidentally flooded the bathroom. Nadine took the opportunity to replace the whole bathroom at a total cost of £5,000. This included £900 that was the cost of repairing the flood damage.

Nadine's property income for 2009/10 is:

	£	£
Rental income		
($£40,000 \times 9/12 + £44,000 \times 3/12$)		41,000
Less: water rates	2,000	
insurance ($£600 \times 9/12 + £800 \times 3/12$)	650	
agents fees	4,100	
repairs	900	
		(7,650)
		33,350

Notes

The rental income and expenses must be dealt with on an accruals basis.

The cost of the flood repairs is allowable because it is a revenue expense. However, the cost of replacing the bathroom is not allowable because this is a capital expense.

Task 1

Harry owns a property that is let for ten weeks from 1 July 2009 at a rent of £160 per week. The tenants leave at the end of this period having paid only £1,300 of the total amount due. Harry writes-off the outstanding debt because the tenants cannot be traced.

The property is re-let to new tenants on 6 March 2010 for a rent of £400 per month payable in arrears (that means at the end of the month). He received the first payment on 10 April 2010.

He paid interest of £700 during the year ended 5 April 2010 on a loan to purchase the property.

Harry's taxable rental income for 2009/10 is:

£ _____

All letting by an individual landlord is treated as a single source of property income. This means that rents and expenses accruing in a tax year on all let properties must be pooled to arrive at a single figure for property income. The effect of this rule is that if the landlord lets several properties he can set-off the running expenses incurred on empty properties (eg properties under repair between lets), against property income generally.

HOW IT WORKS

Bahrat lets two properties in 2009/10. Property 1 was bought in June 2009 and let from 1 July 2009 at an annual rent of £18,000 per annum. Buildings insurance of £8,000 was paid for the year to 30 June 2010. £1,200 was spent in May 2009 on advertising for tenants. Property 2 became vacant on 5 April 2009. Bahrat then spent £5,000 on repairing the leaking roof in the property. The property was let again with effect from 1 March 2010 for £24,000 per annum payable monthly in advance. Buildings insurance of £1,800 was incurred for the year to 31 March 2010.

Bahrat's property income for 2009/10 is:

	£	£
Rental income – property one		
(9/12 × £18,000)		13,500
Rental income – property two		
(1/12 × £24,000)		2,000
Less: buildings insurance (9/12 × £8,000)	6,000	
advertising for tenants	1,200	
repairs	5,000	
buildings insurance	1,800	
		(14,000)
Property income		1,500

Note that a loss would have arisen on property two if it had been dealt with separately. Pooling income and expenses on all let properties effectively allows a loss on one property to be set against income from other properties.

Task 2

Johnson owns two properties:

Whitehouse – let at a rental of £14,000 a year, payable quarterly in advance. The tenant was late in paying the last quarter's rent for the quarter to 5 April 2010 and Johnson did not receive payment until 25 April 2010.

Blackhouse – let at a rent of £6,800 a year payable quarterly in advance. Blackhouse was not let throughout 2008/09; however, a tenant moved in on 24 December 2009.

Johnson pays agents fees of 15% in respect of both properties to his managing agent. He has also incurred the following expenses:

		Whitehouse	Blackhouse
		£	£
Buildings insurance	– year to 30 June 2009	1,200	980
	– year to 30 June 2010	1,400	1,100
Advertising for tenants		–	450

What is Johnson's taxable rental income for 2009/10?

Depreciation on plant and machinery used in the letting business is never allowable, as capital allowances (a form of depreciation for tax purposes) are given instead. You will never be expected to compute capital allowances but you may be given a figure for capital allowances that you are expected to deduct in computing the property income.

Capital allowances are not allowed on furniture used in a property where the tenant lives. Instead, relief for such capital expenditure is given in one of two ways.

The first way is called the RENEWALS BASIS. Here the original cost and the cost of any improvements are not allowable expenditure, but the cost of replacing furniture to the same standard is allowed.

As the renewals basis is cumbersome to administer, many taxpayers use the second way, which is to claim a WEAR AND TEAR ALLOWANCE. This allowance is equal to:

10% [rents – (water rates & council tax if paid by the landlord)]

HOW IT WORKS

Polly lets out a furnished property for £8,000 a year. She pays insurance of £300 per annum and water rates of £400 per annum. Polly chooses to claim the wear and tear allowance in respect of her furniture. Polly's property income for 2009/10 is:

	£	£
Rental income		8,000
Less insurance	300	
water rates	400	
wear and tear allowance		
(10% × £(8,000 – 400)	760	
		(1,460)
Property income		6,540

Task 3

Sunita lets out a furnished property for £12,000 per annum. In 2009/10 she pays water rates of £800 and council tax of £900. She also pays an agent's fee of 10% of rent to the agent who manages the letting.

Sunita chooses to claim the wear and tear allowance in respect of her furniture.

Sunita's taxable property income for 2009/10 is:

A   £8,070
B   £7,900
C   £9,100
D   £9,270

LOSSES

If a landlord makes an overall loss from the letting of properties, there is no liability to tax on property income in that tax year.

The loss is carried forward and set against property income of the following year and subsequent years until the loss is completely used up.

HOW IT WORKS

Maria lets out a house at 30 Thames Drive. Her accrued income and allowable expenses are as follows:

	Income £	Expenses £
2009/10	5,000	12,000
2010/11	7,000	3,000
2011/12	15,000	6,000

The property income for Maria in all three tax years is:

£

2009/10

£(5,000 – 12,000) = £(7,000)

Taxable property income   Nil

2010/11

£(7,000 – 3,000) = £4,000 less use loss b/f of £(4,000)

Taxable property income   Nil

2011/12

£(15,000 – 6,000) = £9,000 less use rest of loss £(3,000)

Taxable property income   6,000

QUALIFYING HOLIDAY ACCOMODATION

There are special rules for the taxation of income arising from qualifying holiday accommodation. This can also be referred to as furnished holiday lettings.

Provided certain conditions are satisfied the following special rules apply:

(a) Losses can be set against other income, not just property income.

(b) The income qualifies as earnings for pension purposes.

(c) Capital allowances are available on furniture. The renewals basis and the wear and tear allowance do not apply if capital allowances are given.

Qualifying holiday accommodation must be:

- Situated in the UK or elsewhere in the EEA; and

- Furnished; and

- Let on a commercial basis with a view to the realisation of profits; and

- Available for letting to the public as holiday accommodation for at least 140 days in the tax year; and

- Actually let for at least 70 days during the same tax year; and

- Not normally occupied for periods of 'longer-term occupation' (more than 31 consecutive days to the same person) for more than 155 days in a tax year.

Where the taxpayer also has other letting income, you must compute furnished holiday letting income separately.

The EEA is the European Economic Area and includes all the countries of the European Union (eg France, Spain) and some other European countries (eg Iceland).

RENT-A-ROOM RELIEF

If an individual lets a furnished room or rooms as living accommodation in his or her main residence, then a special exemption may apply. This is called RENT-A-ROOM RELIEF. The individual may own the residence or himself rent it from a landlord. The relief can apply to lettings in a guest house provided that the house in which the business is carried on is also the taxpayer's main residence.

The limit on the relief is income from the provision of accommodation (before any expenses or capital allowances) of £4,250 a year. This limit is halved if any other person also receives income from renting accommodation in the property. The income to be taken into account includes charges for additional services such as laundry. Capital costs such as the provision of furniture are not included.

If the rental income before expenses is £4,250 or less, the rental income is wholly exempt from income tax but the expenses are ignored. However, the taxpayer may elect not to use rent-a-room relief, for example to make a loss by taking into account both rent and expenses. It only applies for the tax year for which it is made. This election must be made by the 31 January that is 22 months from the end of the tax year concerned.

If gross rents exceed the relevant limit, the taxpayer will be taxed in the ordinary way, ignoring rent-a-room relief, unless he makes an election to use rent-a-room relief. If he makes the election, he will be taxable on gross receipts less £4,250 (or £2,125 if the limit is halved), with no deductions for expenses.

An election to use rent-a-room relief if gross rents exceed the limit must be made by the 31 January that is 22 months from the end of the tax year concerned. The election remains in force until it is withdrawn or until a year in which gross rents do not exceed the limit.

HOW IT WORKS

Sylvia owns a house near the sea in Norfolk. She has a spare bedroom and during 2009/10 this was let to a chef working at a nearby restaurant for £85 per week, which includes the cost of heating, lighting etc. Sylvia estimates that the extra expenses of these amount to £125 per year.

Sylvia has a choice:

(1) Elect for rent-a-room relief: total rental income of £85 × 52 = £4,420 exceeds £4,250 limit so taxable property income is £170 (ie 4,420 – 4,250)

(2) Alternatively, she can be taxed on her actual profit:

	£
Rental income	4,420
Less: expenses	(125)
Taxable property income	4,295

Sylvia should elect to use the rent-a-room basis as this will give her a lower amount of taxable property income.

Task 4

Jordan and Merry are brother and sister. They own a house jointly together and rent out one of the rooms to Zach who pays a rent of £80 per week which is split equally between Jordan and Merry. The expenses relating to the letting are £400.

Explain how Jordan and Merry will be taxed in respect of the letting to Zach.

LAND AND PROPERTY TAX FORM PAGES

In your assessment you may be asked to complete the land and property pages that must accompany the income tax return of someone who lets property. Copies of these pages are included at the end of this chapter. Have a look at them now. You will be able to practise completing this form in the Personal Tax Question Bank.

CHAPTER OVERVIEW

- Property income is income that arises from letting out land and buildings, including from buy-to-let investments

- Property income accruing in a tax year is taxed in that year

- Property income is calculated by taking the rental income accrued and deducting allowable revenue expenditure accrued

- If an individual lets more than one property, the rents and expenses accruing on all of the let properties are pooled

- A landlord of furnished property may either use the renewals basis or the wear and tear allowance

- Rental losses must be carried forward and set against future property profits

- Losses from qualifying holiday accommodation can be set against other income

- Income from qualifying holiday accommodation counts as earnings for pension purposes

- Rent a room relief exempts up to £4,250 of property income when an individual rents a furnished room or rooms in his main residence

Keywords

Landlord – someone who rents out a property to another person called a **tenant**

Furnished letting – a letting which includes the use of furniture belonging to the landlord.

Unfurnished letting – is a letting just of the property without furniture

Buy-to-let investment – a property is bought by an individual specifically with the intention of letting it out and, possibly, benefitting from an increase in its capital value in the future

Accruals basis – for taxing rental income means that all rent accruing in a tax year is taxed in that year

Renewals basis – the cost of replacing furniture is allowed as an expense

Wear and tear allowance – equal to 10% (rent – water rates – council tax paid by the landlord). It may be claimed instead of the renewals basis

Qualifying holiday accommodation – furnished accommodation let on commercial terms with a view to realisation of profit for a certain time each year

Rent-a-room relief – exempts all or part of the property income arising from an individual renting out part of his main residence

TEST YOUR LEARNING

Test 1

David buys a property for letting on 1 August 2009 and grants a tenancy to Ethel from 1 December 2009 at £3,600 pa payable quarterly in advance. The rental income taxable in 2009/10 is:

£

Test 2

Catherine rents out a furnished property for £16,000 pa and pays the water rates of £320 and council tax of £780 on the property.

Relief for wear and tear of furnishings is:

A   £1,600
B   £1,490
C   £1,568
D   £1,522

Test 3

John pays buildings insurance premiums for 12 months in advance on 1 October each year to cover all his letting properties. He pays £4,800 in 2008 and £5,200 in 2009.

How much would be allowed against his rental income for 2009/10?

£

Test 4

Fred has let three holiday bungalows during 2009/10, making a net loss. Explain briefly the difference in treating this loss should the accommodation count as qualifying holiday accommodation.

Test 5

Where profits are being made, what is the main income tax advantage of letting qualifying holiday accommodation?

Test 6

Harry owns a property which he lets for the first time on 1 July 2009 at a rent of £4,000 per annum payable monthly in advance.

The first tenants left without notice on 28 February 2010 and the property was re-let to new tenants on 4 April 2010 at a rent of £5,000 per annum payable yearly in advance.

Harry's allowable expenditure was £1,000 in 2009/10.

What is his taxable rental income for 2009/10?

Test 7

What is the maximum rental income in a tax year which is exempt from income tax under the rent-a-room scheme?

A   £2,125
B   £4,250
C   £4,500
D   £6,475

UK property

Tax year 6 April 2009 to 5 April 2010

Your name

Your unique taxpayer reference (UTR)

UK property details

1 Number of properties rented out

2 If all property income ceased in 2009-10 and you do not expect to receive such income in 2010-11, put 'X' in the box

3 If you have any income from property let jointly, put 'X' in the box

4 If you are claiming Rent a Room relief and your rents are £4,250 or less (or £2,125 if let jointly), put 'X' in the box

Furnished holiday lettings in the UK or EEA

Please read pages UKPN 2 to 5 of the *notes* if you have furnished holiday lettings

5 Income - *the amount of rent and any income for services provided to tenants*

£ · 0 0

6 Rent paid, repairs, insurance and costs of services provided - *the total amount*

£ · 0 0

7 Loan interest and other financial costs

£ · 0 0

8 Legal, management and other professional fees

£ · 0 0

9 Other allowable property expenses

£ · 0 0

10 Private use adjustment - *if expenses include any amounts for non-business purposes*

£ · 0 0

11 Balancing charges - *read page UKPN 5 of the notes*

£ · 0 0

12 Capital allowances - *read page UKPN 5 of the notes*

£ · 0 0

13 Profit for the year (if the amount in box 5 + box 10 + box 11 minus (boxes 6 to 9 + box 12) is positive)

£ · 0 0

Furnished holiday lettings losses

Please read pages UKPN 5 and 6 of the *notes* before filling in boxes 14 to 17

14 Loss for the year (if boxes 6 to 9 + box 12 minus (box 5 + box 10 + box 11) is positive)

£ · 0 0

15 Loss set off against other income from property

£ · 0 0

16 Loss set off against 2009-10 total income

£ · 0 0

17 Loss carried back to earlier years

£ · 0 0

Property income

Do not include Real Estate Investment Trust or Property Authorised Investment Funds dividends/distributions here

18 Total rents and other income from property (including any furnished holiday lettings profits in box 13) £ · 0 0	**20** Premiums for the grant of a lease - *from box E on the Working Sheet on page UKPN 7 of the notes.* £ · 0 0
19 Tax taken off any income in box 18 £ · 0 0	**21** Reverse premiums and inducements £ · 0 0

Property expenses

22 Rent, rates, insurance, ground rents etc. £ · 0 0	**25** Legal, management and other professional fees £ · 0 0
23 Property repairs, maintenance and renewals £ · 0 0	**26** Costs of services provided, including wages £ · 0 0
24 Loan interest and other financial costs £ · 0 0	**27** Other allowable property expenses £ · 0 0

Calculating your taxable profit or loss

28 Private use adjustment - *read page UKPN 9 of the notes* £ · 0 0	**35** Rent a Room exempt amount £ · 0 0
29 Balancing charges - *read page UKPN 9 of the notes* £ · 0 0	**36** Adjusted profit for the year - *from box O on the Working Sheet on page UKPN 14* £ · 0 0
30 Annual Investment Allowance £ · 0 0	**37** Loss brought forward used against this year's profits £ · 0 0
31 Business Premises Renovation Allowance (Assisted Areas only) - *read page UKPN 10 of the notes* £ · 0 0	**38** Taxable profit for the year (box 36 minus box 37) £ · 0 0
32 All other capital allowances £ · 0 0	**39** Adjusted loss for the year - *from box O on the Working Sheet on page UKPN 14* £ · 0 0
33 Landlord's Energy Saving Allowance £ · 0 0	**40** Loss set off against 2009-10 total income - *this will be unusual. See notes on page UKPN 14* £ · 0 0
34 10% wear and tear allowance - *for furnished residential accommodation only* £ · 0 0	**41** Loss to carry forward to following year, including unused losses brought forward £ · 0 0

chapter 4:
TAXABLE INCOME

— chapter coverage 📖 —

In this chapter we look at the three types of income: non-savings, savings and dividend income. We also consider what types of income are exempt from income tax.

We see how to compute an individual's taxable income, including how to deduct a personal allowance or age allowance, which is an amount of income that is not taxable. This enables us to compute an individual's taxable income for a tax year.

The topics covered are:

✍ Non-savings, savings and dividend income

✍ Exempt income

✍ Computation of taxable income

NON-SAVINGS, SAVINGS AND DIVIDEND INCOME

Non-savings income

NON-SAVINGS INCOME is all income other than interest and dividends. You have already met employment income and property income, which are the two main sources of non-savings income in Personal Tax. Other types of non-savings income include:

- Trading income: where an individual carries on a business as a sole trader or partner (dealt with in detail in Business Tax)

- Pension income

Savings income

SAVINGS INCOME is interest received for example from a bank or building society. This can be from an investment account or from a fixed rate savings bond.

An individual may receive bank and building society interest net of 20% tax. This means that the bank/building society deducts 20% tax from the payment made to the individual and pays that tax to HMRC on the individual's behalf. Interest on loan stock from companies not listed on a stock exchange (called 'unlisted' or 'unquoted' companies) is also received net of 20% tax.

Interest must be included gross in the income tax computation. This means that if interest is received net, it must be grossed-up before it is included in the income tax computation. For example, interest received of £80 must be grossed-up to £100 (£80 × 100/80).

The tax suffered on the interest income of £20 can be offset against the individual's income tax payable. If it exceeds the tax payable the excess can be repaid. We examine how to compute income tax payable in the next chapter. In the assessment you may be given either the net or the gross amount of interest: read the question carefully. If you are given the net amount (the amount received or credited), you should gross-up the figure as shown above. However, if you are given the gross amount, include the figure you are given in the income tax computation.

Some interest is received gross (without tax at 20% being deducted). Examples are:

- National Savings & Investments (NS&I) interest including interest from Easy Access Savings Account (EASA), Direct Saver Account, Investment Account and Income Bonds (but not Guaranteed Income Bonds nor Guaranteed Growth Bonds (capital bonds) where tax of 20% is deducted at source)

- Interest on government securities (these are also called 'gilts')

- Interest on loan stock from companies listed on a stock exchange (called 'listed' or 'quoted' companies)

Task 1

Jesse receives building society account interest of £160 and £60 from a NS&I investment account. The total amount of interest on which Jesse will be taxable is:

£ | 200

Dividend income

DIVIDEND INCOME is dividends received from a company. Dividends are always received net of a 10% tax credit. This means a dividend received of £90 has a £10 tax credit, giving gross income of £100 to be included in the tax computation. The tax credit attached to dividends cannot be repaid to non-taxpayers but it can be offset against a taxpayer's tax liability. We see how to compute a taxpayer's tax liability in the next chapter.

Task 2

Maria receives dividends of £900 and building society interest of £1,600. What are the gross amounts of dividends and interest to be included in her income tax computation?   1000 + 2000 = 3000

EXEMPT INCOME

Some income which would be taxable as savings or dividend income is exempt from income tax. You must not include this income in the income tax computation.

In your assessment you should always state if income is exempt. If you do not, you may not be awarded the available mark.

Individual savings account

An individual savings account (ISA) is a special tax exempt way of saving. In 2009/10 an individual aged 50 or under can invest £7,200 in ISAs, of which up to £3,600 can be held as cash. Individuals who are aged 50 or over in 2009/10 can invest £10,200 in ISAs, of which up to £5,100 can be held as cash. Funds invested in ISAs can be used to buy stock market investments, units in unit trusts, fixed interest investments, or insurance policies. Dividends and interest received from ISAs are exempt from income tax, whether paid out to the investor or retained and reinvested within the ISA.

NS&I Savings Certificates

Savings certificates are issued by National Savings and Investments (NS&I). They may be fixed rate certificates or index linked and are for fixed terms of between two and five years. On maturity the profit is tax exempt. This profit is often called interest.

Task 3

Denis receives the following (cash amounts)

Dividends in ISA	£360
Interest on maturity of NS&I	
Savings certificates	£180
Interest from NatWest Bank deposit a/c	£80

The total taxable interest assessable on Denis is:

A   £280
B   £665
C   £100 ✓
D   £680

Other exempt income

Other exempt income includes:

- Damages for personal injury or death
- Scholarships and educational grants (exempt as income of the student. If paid by a parent's employer, a scholarship may be taxable income of the parent)
- Prizes, lotto winnings, gambling winnings
- Premium Bond prizes

COMPUTATION OF TAXABLE INCOME

Computing total income

For each tax year, an individual may receive various 'components' of income. All income must be brought together in a personal tax computation and is called TOTAL INCOME.

In the personal tax computation income must be split into three types:

(a) Non-savings income
(b) Savings income
(c) Dividend income

HOW IT WORKS

In 2009/10, Margaret earns a salary of £30,000, receives gross interest of £1,000 and gross dividends of £1,000.

Her total income computation is:

	Non-savings income £	Savings income £	Dividend income £	Total £
Employment income	30,000			
Interest		1,000		
UK dividends			1,000	
Total income	30,000	1,000	1,000	32,000

Task 4

Tracey has the following types of income in 2009/10.

	£
Business income	44,000
Building society interest (gross)	2,000
Dividends (gross)	1,000
Lotto winnings	10

Show her total income split into non-savings, savings and dividend income.

44,000

2,000
2,000

1,000
47,000

Personal allowance

All persons (including children) who are under the age of 65 at 5 April 2010 are entitled to a personal allowance (PA) of £6,475 in 2009/10.

The personal allowance (or the age allowance – see below) is deducted from total income to arrive at TAXABLE INCOME. The allowance is deducted first from non-savings income, then from savings income, and any remaining allowance from dividend income.

HOW IT WORKS

In 2009/10, Joe, who is aged 25, has trade profits of £3,000, receives bank interest of £14,000 and dividends of £450. Joe's taxable income for 2009/10 is:

	Non-savings income £	Savings income £	Dividend income £	Total £
Trade profits	3,000			
Building society interest (× 100/80)		17,500		
Dividends (× 100/90)			500	
Total income	3,000	17,500	500	21,000
Less: personal allowance	(3,000)	(3,475)	–	
Taxable income	–	14,025	500	14,525

Task 5

John, who is aged 46, has trade profits of £10,000 in 2009/10. He also received building society interest of £2,000, premium bond prizes of £250 and dividends of £4,500. Show John's taxable income for 2009/10.

Age allowance

A person aged 65–74 is entitled to an age allowance of £9,490 instead of the personal allowance of £6,475. A person aged 75 or over receives a higher age allowance of £9,640 instead of the personal allowance of £6,475.

If the individual's net income exceeds £22,900 the age allowance is reduced by £1 for each £2 by which total income exceeds £22,900. The age allowance cannot be reduced below £6,475.

An individual is entitled to the age allowance, or higher age allowance, provided he attains the age of 65 or 75 respectively before the end of the tax year, or would have had he not died before his birthday.

HOW IT WORKS

In 2009/10, Keith, who is aged 73, has gross pension income of £18,000, receives building society interest of £1,600, damages of £1,500 for personal injury following a fall and dividends of £3,600. Keith's taxable income for 2009/10 is:

	Non-savings income	Savings income	Dividend income	Total
	£	£	£	£
Pension income	18,000			
Building society interest (× 100/80)		2,000		
Dividends (× 100/90)			4,000	
Total income	18,000	2,000	4,000	24,000
Less age allowance (W)	(8,940)	–	–	
Taxable income	9,060	2,000	4,000	15,060

Working

	£
Total income	24,000
Less: income limit	(22,900)
Excess	1,100
Age allowance	9,490
Less: half excess	(550)
Amount available	8,940

Task 6

In 2009/10, Zebedee, who is aged 80, has pension income of £17,500, receives bank interest of £2,000 and dividends of £4,500. The age allowance that Zebedee is entitled to in 2009/10 is:

£ 8,590

There is also special rule relating to the calculation of age allowance where the taxpayer has made;

(a) A Gift Aid donation, or

(b) A contribution to a personal pension scheme

during the tax year. We will look at these payments in more detail in the next chapter and you may want to review this rule after studying that chapter.

The rule is that, for the purposes of comparing total income with the income limit of £22,900, total income is reduced by the gross amount of the Gift Aid donations and personal pension contributions.

HOW IT WORKS

Millie is aged 68. In 2009/10, she has total income of £26,500. Millie also makes a personal pension contribution of £2,000 (gross) in 2009/10.

Millie's age allowance is calculated as follows:

	£
Total income	26,500
Less: personal pension contribution	(2,000)
Adjusted total income	24,500
Less: income limit	(22,900)
Excess	1,600
Age allowance	9,490
Less: half excess	(800)
Adjusted age allowance	7,890

Task 7

Ernest is aged 82. His total income in 2009/10 is £29,000 and he makes a Gift Aid donation of £500 (gross) in January 2010.

Ernest is entitled to an age allowance in 2009/10 of:

£ [   ]

CHAPTER OVERVIEW

- There are three types of income: non-savings, savings and dividend

- Non-savings income includes employment income, property income, trading income and pension income

- Savings income is interest

- If an individual receives interest net of 20% tax it must be grossed-up by multiplying by 100/80

- Dividends are received net of a 10% tax credit. Gross dividends up by multiplying by 100/90

- Exempt income includes income from individual savings accounts, NS&I Savings Certificates and gambling winnings

- Tax computations must be prepared for a tax year

- All the components of an individual's income are added together to arrive at 'total income'

- Total income less the personal allowance or age allowance leaves you 'taxable income'

- The personal allowance is deducted first from non-savings income, then from savings income and finally from dividend income

- The age allowance is given to individuals aged 65 or over at the end of the tax year. It is reduced by £1 for every £2 that the individual's income exceeds the income limit, but cannot be less than the personal allowance

- The income limit for age allowance is reduced by gross Gift Aid donations and personal pension contributions

Keywords

Non-savings income – income other than interest and dividends

Savings income – interest

Dividend income – dividends received

Total income – the total of an individual's income from all sources

Taxable income – an individual's total income minus the personal allowance or the age allowance

TEST YOUR LEARNING

Test 1

Classify the following types of income by ticking the correct box:

	Non-savings income	Savings income	Dividend income
Employment income	☑	☐	☐
Dividend received	☐	☐	☑
Property income	☑	☐	☐
Bank interest	☐	☑	☐
Pension income	☑	☐	☐
Interest on government stock	☐	☑	☐

Test 2

What amounts must be included in the personal tax computation in respect of the following:

(a) Building society interest received of £240 ~ £300
(b) Interest received on an individual savings account of £40 £60
(c) Dividends received of £144 £160

Test 3

Joe has employment income of £30,000 and receives dividends of £270 in 2009/10 and interest of £250 on the maturity of his NS&I Savings Certificates. Show his taxable income for 2009/10.

Test 4

Pratish receives property income of £3,000 and building society interest of £7,200 in 2009/10. What is his taxable income for 2009/10?

Test 5

Jesse has employment income of £20,000 in 2009/10. He also received building society interest of £4,000, a prize of £50 in an internet competition and dividends of £3,600. What is Jesse's taxable income for 2009/10?

Test 6

Zoreen has her 75th birthday on 10 May 2009. In 2009/10, she receives pension income of £18,380, bank interest of £4,000 and dividends of £5,400.

What is the age allowance available to Zoreen for 2009/10?

A   £9,640
B   £6,400
C   £6,475 ✓
D   £9,490

Test 7

Escamillo is aged 69. In 2009/10, he receives pension income of £25,400 and makes a gross gift aid donation of £1,000.

What is the age allowance available to Escamillo for 2009/10?

A   £9,640
B   £9,190
C   £8,690
D   £9,490

chapter 5:
CALCULATION OF INCOME TAX

chapter coverage 📖

In the last chapter you saw how to compute an individual's taxable income. In this chapter you will see how to compute the income tax payable on this income.

The topics covered are:

✎ Calculating the income tax liability

✎ Calculating income tax payable

CALCULATING THE INCOME TAX LIABILITY

Income tax bands

In the last chapter we saw how to compute taxable income. We now see how to compute the income tax liability on this taxable income.

First, the taxable income needs to be divided into two bands:

(a) The first £37,400 of income; this is income in the BASIC RATE BAND
(b) The remaining income over the HIGHER RATE THRESHOLD of £37,400

The rate of tax applied to the income in each band depends on whether the income is non-savings income, savings income or dividend income.

There is only one set of income tax bands used for all three types of income. These bands must be allocated to income in the following order:

(a) Non-savings income
(b) Savings income
(c) Dividend income

There is a special rule where the taxpayer has little or no non-savings income but has savings income. We deal with this later in this chapter.

Computing the tax liability

You need to calculate the tax due on taxable income as follows:

(1) **Deal with non-savings income first**

Non-savings income in the basic rate band is taxed at 20%. Non-savings income above the higher rate threshold is taxed at 40%.

(2) **Second, deal with savings income**

Savings income is dealt with after non-savings income. If any of the basic rate band remains after taxing non-savings income it can be used here.

Savings income that falls within the basic rate band is taxed at 20%. Once savings income is above the higher rate threshold, it is taxed at 40%.

(3) **Third, compute tax on dividend income**

Last, tax dividend income. If dividend income falls within the basic rate band, it is taxed at 10% (not 20%). If, however, the dividend income exceeds the higher rate threshold of £37,400, it is taxed at 32.5%.

(4) **Total the tax – tax liability**

Add the above three amounts of tax together. The resulting figure is the income tax liability.

HOW IT WORKS

Sasha has taxable income of £42,300. Of this, £35,500 is non-savings income, £3,000 is savings income and £3,800 is dividend income.

The non-savings income of £35,500 is all in the basic rate band. £1,900 of the interest uses the remaining basic rate band. £1,100 of interest and all the dividends are above the higher rate threshold of £37,400.

The tax liability is:

		Income tax
		£
(1)	**Non-savings income**	
	£35,500 × 20%	7,100.00
(2)	**Savings income**	
	<u>£1,900</u> × 20%	380.00
	£37,400	
	£1,100 × 40%	440.00
(3)	**Dividend income**	
	<u>£3,800</u> × 32.5%	1,235.00
	<u>£42,300</u>	
(4)	**Tax liability**	9,155.00

Task 1

Talet has taxable income of £60,000 for 2009/10. £25,000 of her taxable income is non-savings income. The remaining £35,000 is savings income. What is her income tax liability?

£ 16520

Savings income starting rate

There is a special rule where the taxpayer has little or no non-savings income but has savings income.

In this case, there is a starting rate of 10% for the first £2,440 of savings income. This is called the SAVINGS INCOME STARTING RATE BAND.

The savings income starting rate only applies where savings income falls within the savings income starting rate band. Remember that income tax is charged first on non-savings income. In most cases, an individual's non-savings income will exceed the savings income starting rate band, which will mean that savings income will fall in the basic rate band.

However, if an individual's non-savings income does not use up the savings income starting rate band, then savings income will be taxable at the 10% savings income starting rate within that band.

HOW IT WORKS

Tamara has taxable income of £10,000 in 2009/10. £2,000 is non-savings income and £8,000 is savings income. Her income tax liability is:

	Income tax £
Non-savings income	
£2,000 × 20%	400.00
Savings income	
£(2,440 – 2,000) = £440 × 10%	44.00
£(8,000 – 440) = £7,560 × 20%	1,512.00
Income tax liability	1,956.00

Task 2

In 2009/10, Joe earns a salary of £7,000 from a part-time job and receives bank interest of £4,000. Joe's income tax liability for 2009/10 is:

£ 913.50

Extending the basic rate band

We have seen above that an individual normally has a basic rate band of £37,400 in 2009/10. There are two circumstances in which the basic rate band must be increased. These are when the individual pays:

(a) A Gift Aid donation, or
(b) A contribution to a personal pension scheme

A Gift Aid donation is a particular type of donation to charity on which tax relief is available.

Both Gift Aid donations and contributions to personal pension schemes are paid net of 20% tax. For example, this means that if an individual pays a Gift Aid donation of £800, the gross amount of the donation is £800 × 100/80 = £1,000.

An individual obtains basic rate tax relief on Gift Aid donations and personal pension contributions by paying them net. If the individual is a basic rate taxpayer, no further adjustments need to be made.

If the taxpayer is liable to tax at the higher rate, additional relief is given. However, this must take account of the fact that basic rate relief has already been given. The way this is done is to extend the basic rate band by the gross amount of a Gift Aid donation and/or the gross amount of any personal pension contribution paid. This means that the gross payment will be taxed at the basic rate but will not be taxed at the higher rate.

HOW IT WORKS

Gustav has taxable income (all non-savings) of £50,000 in 2009/10.

Assuming that Gustav does not make any Gift Aid donations nor personal pension contributions in 2009/10, his income tax liability will be:

	£
£37,400 × 20%	7,480.00
£12,600 × 40%	5,040.00
£50,000	12,520.00

Now think about the situation where Gustav makes a Gift Aid donation of £8,000 in 2009/10. The Gift Aid donation will have been paid net of 20% tax. This means that the gross amount of the payment is £8,000 × 100/80 = £10,000 and Gustav's basic rate band must be extended by £10,000. His income tax liability is calculated as follows:

	£
£37,400 × 20%	7,480.00
£10,000 (extended band) × 20%	2,000.00
£2,600 × 40%	1,040.00
50,000	10,520.00

The difference between the tax liabilities without and with the Gift Aid donation is £10,000 × (40 − 20)% = £2,000. The total tax relief is:

	£
Basic rate relief given by net payment	2,000.00
Higher rate relief given by extending basic rate band	2,000.00
Total tax relief	4,000.00

Task 3

In 2009/10 Hans has taxable income of £50,000. £24,000 of this income is non-savings income, the rest is savings income. Hans pays a personal pension contribution of £5,600 in 2009/10. Hans' tax liability for 2009/10 is:

A	£10,000
B	£11,400
C	£12,520
D	£11,120

CALCULATING INCOME TAX PAYABLE

We have seen above how to calculate the income tax liability on non-savings, savings and dividend income. Once this is done there are two final adjustments to be made in order to arrive at the tax payable, which is the balance of the liability still to be settled in cash.

(1) Deduct the tax credit on dividends from the tax liability. Although deductible, this tax credit cannot be repaid if it exceeds the income tax liability.

Task 4

Doris received dividend income of £22,500 in 2009/10. She has no other income. The tax payable is:

£	Nil

(2) Finally deduct any tax deducted at source on savings income, and any tax deducted under the PAYE system by an employer.

These amounts of tax suffered can be repaid to the extent that they exceed the income tax liability.

HOW IT WORKS

Samantha has the following income and outgoings for 2009/10.

	£
Salary (tax deducted by employer £4,000)	25,000
UK dividend received (net)	2,000
Building society interest received (net)	16,400
Qualifying charitable donations paid under Gift Aid	
(gross amount)	300

Samantha's tax payable for 2009/10 is:

	Non-savings income £	Savings income £	Dividend income £	Total £
Employment income	25,000			
Building Society interest				
£16,400 × 100/80		20,500		
UK dividends				
£2,000 × 100/90			2,222	
Total income	25,000	20,500	2,222	47,722
Less: personal allowance	(6,475)			
Taxable income	18,525	20,500	2,222	41,247

	£
Tax on non-savings income	
£18,525 × 20%	3,705.00
Tax on savings income	
£18,875 £(37,400 – 18,525) × 20%	3,775.00
£300 × 20%	60.00
£1,325 × 40%	530.00
Tax on dividend income	
£2,222 × 32.5%	722.15
	8,792.15
Less: tax credit on dividend income (£2,222 × 10%)	(222.00)
Less: income tax suffered	
tax on employment income 4,000.00	
tax on interest (£20,500 × 20%) 4,100.00	
	(8,100.00)
Income tax payable	470.15

Note. The basic rate band is extended by the gross amount of the Gift Aid donation.

Task 5

In 2009/10 Barry has rental income of £31,000, bank interest (net amount received) of £8,000, and UK dividends received of £10,800. Compute Barry's income tax payable for 2009/10.

£ 6958.13

Task 6

Kate, who is aged 66, has a salary of £14,955 (tax deducted by employer £900) and building society interest received of £4,000. Calculate Kate's tax payable for 2009/10.

19,995
‿ 6475
_____
13480
‿ 6475
_____
7005   (9 2⁰

14955
‿ 6475
_____
8480
5000

20% = 1696

20%   = 1,000
      _____
      2,696
‿ 1000
_____
7₍₆

CHAPTER OVERVIEW

- We categorise income into different types: non-savings; savings and dividend. Each type of income suffers different rates of tax depending on whether the income falls into the basic or higher rate band

- Non-savings income is taxed first (at 20% then 40%) then savings income (at 20% then 40%) and finally dividend income (at 10% and 32.5%)

- The savings income starting rate of 10% applies to savings income within the savings income starting rate band

- Gift Aid donations and personal pension contributions are paid net of basic rate (20%) tax

- Extend the basic rate band by the gross amount of any Gift Aid donations or personal pension contributions paid. This gives additional tax relief to higher rate taxpayers

- Deduct the tax credit on dividend income from the income tax liability. However, if it exceeds the income tax liability, the excess cannot be repaid

- Tax suffered on interest and tax deducted under the PAYE system is deducted in computing tax payable and can be repaid

Keywords

Basic rate band – the first £37,400 of income. The basic rate band may be extended by the gross amount of any Gift Aid donations and personal pension contributions paid

Higher rate threshold – is the threshold over which income is taxed at the higher rate

Savings rate starting band – applies if the taxpayer does not have non-savings income of at least this amount but has savings income

TEST YOUR LEARNING

Test 1

At what rates is income tax charged on non-savings income?

A   10%, 20% and 40%
B   40% only
C   20% only
D   20% and 40%

Test 2

In 2009/10, Albert has a salary of £12,000, £2,000 (gross) of building society interest and £3,000 (gross) of UK dividends. Albert's income tax liability is:

£   1805

Test 3

In 2009/10 Carol has a salary of £4,000, and has received building society interest of £14,400 and a UK dividend of £19,800. Carol's income tax liability is:

£   5089.13

Test 4

Explain how tax relief is given on Gift Aid donations.   Net   Set
   Gross
8 given higher tax life

Test 5

Doreen, who is aged 80, has the following sources of income in 2009/10.

	£	
Pension income (tax deducted under PAYE £2,100)	17,000	- 1502
Property income	3,500	700
Interest received from NS&I Investment account	380	70
UK dividends received	630	
Premium bond prize	100	

Calculate Doreen's income tax payable for the year.   172

Test 6

Sase has the following income and outgoings in 2009/10.

	£
Business profits	38,000
Building society interest received	4,000
UK dividends received	3,600
Gift Aid donation paid	1,600

Compute Sase's income tax payable for the year.

£6558.16

chapter 6:
SELF-ASSESSMENT
OF INCOME TAX

chapter coverage 📖

In this chapter we look at when tax returns must be filed, for how long records must be kept, and at the penalties chargeable for failure to comply with the requirements.

We then look at the due dates for payment of income tax and the consequences of late payment.

Finally, we consider the important topic of client confidentiality.

The topics covered are:

✍ Tax returns and keeping records

✍ Penalties

✍ Payment of tax, interest and surcharges

✍ Enquiries

4000

18000

22000

4000	18000		44000
	52475		G 6475
4000	75525		37525
NIL			

$2440 \times 10\% = 244$

$13065 \times 20\% = 2617$

$21975 \times 10\% = 2187.50$

$125 \times 32.5\% = 40.63$

5064.13

TAX RETURNS AND KEEPING RECORDS

An individual's tax return comprises a Tax Form, together with supplementary pages for particular sources of income and chargeable gains . You may have to complete the supplementary employment or the supplementary land and property pages in your assessment. These forms were included for you to look at earlier in this Text. You will be able to practise completing them in the Personal Tax Question Bank. We will look at chargeable gains and self assessment later in this Text.

Notice of chargeability

Individuals who are chargeable to tax for any tax year and who have not received a notice to file a return are, in general, required to give notice of chargeability within six months from the end of the year, ie by 5 October 2010 for 2009/10.

Filing tax returns

The FILING DUE DATE is:

- For paper returns – 31 October following the end of the tax year that the return covers, eg for 2009/10 by 31 October 2010.

- For returns filed online – 31 January following the end of the tax year that the return covers, eg for 2009/10 by 31 January 2011.

Where a notice to make a return is issued after 31 October following the tax year, a period of three months is allowed for the online filing of that return. Where a notice to make a return is issued after 31 July following the tax year, a period of three months is allowed for the filing of a paper return.

An individual may ask HMRC to make the tax computation if a paper return is filed. Where an online return is filed, the tax computation is made automatically.

HOW IT WORKS

Advise the following clients of the latest filing date for their personal tax return for 2009/10 if the return is:

(a) Paper

(b) Online

Norma   Notice to file tax return issued by HMRC on 6 April 2010

Melanie   Notice to file tax return issued by HMRC on 10 August 2010

Olga   Notice to file tax return issued by HMRC on 12 December 2010

The latest filing dates are:

	Paper	**Online**
Norma	31 October 2010	31 January 2011
Melanie	9 November 2010	31 January 2011
Olga	11 March 2011	11 March 2011

Task 1

HMRC issued a notice to file a tax return for 2009/10 to Myer on 3 November 2010. She filed this return online on 31 March 2010. State the date by which the return should have been filed:

[handwritten:)8)2.]

Keeping of records

Taxpayers must keep and retain all records required to enable them to make and deliver a correct tax return.

In general, records must be retained by tax payers until the later of:

(a) One year after the 31 January following the tax year concerned

(b) Five years after 31 January following the tax year concerned if the taxpayer is in business or has property business income

PENALTIES

Penalties for error

A penalty may be imposed where a taxpayer makes an inaccurate return if he has:

(a) Been careless because he has not taken reasonable care in making the return or discovers the error later but does not take reasonable steps to inform HMRC

(b) Made a deliberate error but does not make arrangements to conceal it

(c) Made a deliberate error and has attempted to conceal it, eg by submitting false evidence in support of an inaccurate figure

An error that is made where the taxpayer has taken reasonable care in making the return and which he does not discover later, does not result in a penalty.

In order for a penalty to be charged, the inaccurate return must result in:

(a) An understatement of the taxpayer's tax liability; or

    (b)   A false or increased loss for the taxpayer; or

    (c)   A false or increased repayment of tax to the taxpayer

If a return contains more than one error, a penalty can be charged for each error. The rules also extend to errors in claims for allowances and reliefs and in accounts submitted in relation to tax liability.

The amount of the penalty for error is based on the Potential Lost Revenue (PLR) to HMRC as a result of the error. For example, if there is an understatement of tax, this understatement will be the PLR.

The maximum amount of the penalty for error depends on the type of error.

Type of error	Maximum penalty payable
Careless	30% of PLR
Deliberate not concealed	70% of PLR
Deliberate and concealed	100% of PLR

A penalty for error may be reduced if the taxpayer tells HMRC about the error – this is called a disclosure. The reduction depends on the circumstances of the disclosure and the help that the taxpayer gives to HMRC in relation to the disclosure.

An unprompted disclosure is one made at a time when the taxpayer has no reason to believe HMRC has discovered, or is about to discover, the error. Otherwise, the disclosure will be a prompted disclosure. The minimum penalties that can be imposed are as follows.

Type of error	Unprompted	Prompted
Careless	0% of PLR	15% of PLR
Deliberate not concealed	20% of PLR	35% of PLR
Deliberate and concealed	30% of PLR	50% of PLR

You will see that an unprompted disclosure where a careless mistake has been made can reduce a penalty for error to nil, and all penalties can be reduced by half if the taxpayer makes a prompted disclosure.

A penalty for a careless error may be suspended by HMRC to allow the taxpayer to take action to ensure that the error does not occur again (eg where the error has arisen from failure to keep proper records).

HMRC will impose conditions which the taxpayer has to satisfy, eg establishing proper recordkeeping systems.

The penalty will be cancelled if the conditions imposed by HMRC are complied with by the taxpayer within a period of up to two years.

A taxpayer can appeal against:

    (a)   The penalty being charged

    (b)   The amount of the penalty

    (c)   A decision by HMRC not to suspend a penalty

    (d)   The conditions set by HMRC in relation to the suspension of a penalty

Penalties for late notification

A penalty can be charged for failure to notify chargeability to income tax and/or capital gains tax that results in a loss of tax. Penalties are behaviour related, increasing for more serious failures, and are based on Potential Lost Revenue.

The minimum and maximum penalties as percentages of PLR are as follows:

Behaviour	Maximum penalty	Minimum penalty with unprompted disclosure		Minimum penalty with prompted disclosure	
Deliberate and concealed	100%	30%		50%	
Deliberate but not concealed	70%	20%		35%	
		>12m	<12m	>12m	<12m
Careless	30%	10%	0%	20%	10%

There is no zero penalty for reasonable care (as there is for penalties for errors on returns – see above), although the penalty may be reduced to 0% if the failure is rectified within 12 months through unprompted disclosure. The penalties may also be reduced at HMRC's discretion in 'special circumstances'. Inability to pay the penalty is not a 'special circumstance'.

The same penalties apply for failure to notify HMRC of a new taxable activity.

Where the taxpayer's failure is not 'deliberate', there is no penalty if he can show he has a 'reasonable excuse'. Reasonable excuse does not include having insufficient money to pay the penalty. Taxpayers can appeal against penalty decisions.

Penalties for late filing

The maximum penalties for filing a late tax return are:

    (a)   Return up to six months late: £100

    (b)   Return more than six months but not more than 12 months late: £200

    (c)   Return more than twelve months late: £200 + 100% of the tax liability

In addition, a maximum penalty of £60 per day can be imposed where failure to deliver a tax return continues after notice has been given to the taxpayer. In this case the additional £100 penalty, imposed under (b) if the return is more than six months late, is not charged.

The fixed penalties of £100/£200 can be set aside if the taxpayer had a reasonable excuse for not delivering the return. If the tax liability shown on the return is less than the fixed penalties, the fixed penalty is reduced to the amount of the tax liability. The tax-geared penalty can also be reduced.

Penalties for failure to keep records

The maximum penalty for each failure to keep and retain records is £3,000.

PAYMENT OF TAX, INTEREST AND SURCHARGES

Payments of tax

A taxpayer must make three payments of income tax:

Date	Payment
31 January in the tax year	First payment on account
31 July after the tax year	Second payment on account
31 January after the tax year	Final payment to settle any remaining liability

Each PAYMENT ON ACCOUNT is equal to 50% of the income tax payable (after the deduction of tax suffered at source) for the previous year.

Capital gains tax must all be paid on 31 January following the tax year. There are no payments on account of capital gains tax.

HOW IT WORKS

Jeremy paid tax for 2009/10 as follows:

	£
Income tax payable	12,000
Capital gains tax payable	2,000

The payments on account for 2010/11 are:

The income tax payable for 2009/10 was £12,000

Each payment on account is £12,000/2 = £6,000

Task 2

Karen paid tax for 2009/10 as follows:

	£
Income tax payable	14,000
Capital gains tax	8,000

What payments on account must Karen make for 2010/11?

Payments on account are not required if the income tax payable for the previous year is less than £1,000.

Payments on account are normally fixed by reference to the previous year's tax liability but if a taxpayer expects his liability to be lower than this he may claim to reduce his payments on account to:

(a) A stated amount
(b) Nil

If the taxpayer's eventual liability is higher than he estimated he will have reduced the payments on account too far. Although the payments on account will not be adjusted, the taxpayer will suffer an interest charge on late payment.

The balance of any income tax is normally payable on or before the 31 January following the year.

HOW IT WORKS

Jameel made payments on account for 2009/10 of £7,500 each on 31 January 2010 and 31 July 2010, based on his 2008/09 liability. He later calculates his total income tax payable for 2009/10 at £20,000.

The final payment for 2009/10 is calculated as follows:

	£
Income tax (£20,000 – £7,500 – £7,500)	5,000
Capital gains tax	4,900
Final payment	9,900

In one case the due date for the final payment is later than 31 January following the end of the year. If a taxpayer has notified chargeability by 5 October but the notice to file a tax return is not issued before 31 October, then the due date for the payment is three months after the issue of the notice.

Surcharges

SURCHARGES are normally imposed in respect of balancing payments of income tax and any CGT.

	Paid	**Surcharge**
(a)	Within 28 days of due date:	none
(b)	More than 28 days but not more than six months after the due date:	5%
(c)	More than six months after the due date:	10%

Surcharges apply to balancing payments of income tax and any CGT. The surcharges do not apply to late payments on account.

Interest

INTEREST is chargeable on late payment of both payments on account and balancing payments. In both cases interest runs from the due date until the day before the actual date of payment.

If a taxpayer claims to reduce his payments on account and there is still a final payment to be made, interest is normally charged on the payments on account as if each of those payments had been the lower of:

(a) The reduced amount, plus 50% of the final income tax liability

(b) The amount which would have been payable had no claim for reduction been made

HOW IT WORKS

Harry made two payments on account of £2,500 each for 2009/10. The payments were made on 31 January 2010 and 31 July 2010. Harry had claimed to reduce these payments from the £4,000 that would have been due had they been based on his previous year's income tax liability.

Harry's 2009/10 tax return showed that his tax liabilities for 2009/10 (before deducting payments on account) were income tax: £10,000; capital gains tax: £3,000. Harry paid the balance of tax due of £8,000 on 30 September 2011.

Harry will be charged interest as follows:

The payments on account should have been £4,000 each. Interest will therefore be charged on the £1,500 not paid on 31 January 2010 until the date of payment 30 September 2011. Similarly, interest will run on the other £1,500 that should have been paid on 31 July 2010 until 30 September 2011.

The final balancing payment should have been £13,000 – £8,000 = £5,000. Interest will run on £5,000 from the due date of 31 January 2011 until the date of payment 30 September 2011.

Note. There would also be a surcharge of 10% due on the balancing payment.

Repayment of tax and repayment supplement

Tax is repaid when claimed unless a greater payment of tax is due in the following 30 days, in which case it is set-off against that payment.

Interest is paid on overpayments of:

(a) Payments on account
(b) Final payments of income tax and CGT
(c) Penalties and surcharges

Interest runs from the original date of payment (even if this was prior to the due date), until the day before the date the repayment is made.

Repayment supplement is interest payable on overpaid tax. However for 2009/10 the rate of repayment supplement is 0%.

ENQUIRIES

HMRC can enquire into a return if it gives written notice within one year of:

(a) The actual filing date (if the return was filed on or before the due filing date)

(b) 31 January, 30 April, 31 July or 31 October following the actual filing date (if the return was filed after the due filing date)

A reason for raising an enquiry does not have to be given. In particular, the taxpayer will not be advised whether he has been selected at random for an audit. Enquiries may be full enquiries, or may be limited to 'aspect' enquiries.

In the course of the enquiries the taxpayer may be required to produce documents, accounts or other information. The taxpayer can appeal to the Tax Tribunal against this.

HMRC must issue a closure notice when the enquiries are complete, state the conclusions and amend the self-assessment accordingly. If the taxpayer is not satisfied with the amendment he may, within 30 days, appeal to the Tax Tribunal.

Once an enquiry is complete HMRC cannot make further enquiries. HMRC may, in limited circumstances, raise a discovery assessment if it believes that there has been a loss of tax.

CHAPTER OVERVIEW

- A tax return must be filed by 31 January following a tax year provided it is filed online. Paper returns must be filed by 31 October following the tax year

- A penalty may be imposed if the taxpayer makes an error in his tax return, based on the Potential Loss of Revenue as a result of the error

- A penalty may be imposed if the taxpayer does not notify HMRC of his liability to pay income tax or capital gains tax. The penalty is based on Potential Lost Revenue.

- Fixed penalties of £100/£200 apply if a return is filed up to/more than six months late

- A tax-geared penalty may apply if a return is filed more than 12 months late

- Payments on account of income tax are required on 31 January in the tax year and on 31 July following the tax year

- Balancing payments of income tax and all CGT are due on 31 January following the tax year

- Surcharges apply to balancing payments of income tax or any CGT. The surcharges do not apply to late payments on account

- Interest is chargeable on late payment of both payments on account and balancing payments

- HMRC can enquire into a return within one year of receipt of the return, if it is filed on or before the due filing date

Keywords

Filing due date – the date by which a return must be filed

Payment on account – an amount paid on account of income tax

Surcharges – imposed in respect of balancing payments of income tax and any CGT paid late

Interest – charged on late payments on account and on late balancing payments

TEST YOUR LEARNING

Test 1

What is the due filing date for an income tax return for 2009/10 assuming the taxpayer will submit the return online?

Test 2

How will 2009/10 payments on account be calculated and when are they due?

Test 3

A notice requiring a tax return for 2009/10 is issued in April 2010 and filed online in May 2011. All income tax was paid in May 2011. No payments on account were due. What charges will be made on the taxpayer?

Test 4

Sase filed her 2009/10 tax return online on 28 January 2011. By what date must HMRC give notice that they are going to enquire into the return?

A   31 January 2012
B   31 March 2012
C   6 April 2011
D   28 January 2012

Test 5

Jamie paid income tax of £12,000 for 2008/09. In 2009/10, his tax liability was £16,000.

State when payments must be made in respect of Jamie's 2009/10 income tax liability.

Test 6

Tim should have made two payments on account of his 2009/10 income tax liability of £5,000 each. He actually made both of these payments on 31 August 2010.

State the amount of any surcharges due.

£

chapter 7:
COMPUTING CAPITAL GAINS TAX

chapter coverage 📖

In this chapter we see how to compute chargeable gains or allowable losses arising on the disposal of assets, including part disposals of assets.

We see how to set allowable losses against chargeable gains and how to arrive at the net gains taxable in any particular tax year. Then we note how to compute the capital gains tax payable in any particular tax year.

Finally, we look at the special rules that apply when disposals are made to connected people or between married couples/civil partners.

The topics covered are:

- ✒ When does a chargeable gain arise?
- ✒ Computing chargeable gains and allowable losses
- ✒ Part disposals
- ✒ Computing taxable gains in a tax year
- ✒ Computing capital gains tax payable
- ✒ Self assessment for capital gains tax
- ✒ Connected persons
- ✒ Spouses/civil partners
- ✒ Capital gains summary pages

WHEN DOES A CHARGEABLE GAIN ARISE?

You saw earlier in this Text that, as a general rule, income is a receipt that is expected to recur (such as rental income), whereas a gain is a one-off profit on the disposal of a capital asset (eg the profit on the sale of an investment property). For the gain on the disposal of a capital asset to be a chargeable gain there must be a CHARGEABLE DISPOSAL of a CHARGEABLE ASSET by a CHARGEABLE PERSON.

Chargeable persons

Individuals are the only type of chargeable person that you will meet in Personal Tax.

Chargeable disposals

The following are the most important chargeable disposals:

- Sales of assets or parts of assets
- Gifts of assets or parts of assets

A chargeable disposal occurs on the date of the contract (where there is one, whether written or oral), or the date of a conditional contract becoming unconditional.

The transfer of an asset on death is an EXEMPT DISPOSAL. On death the heirs inherit assets as if they bought them at death for their then market values. There is no capital gain or allowable loss on death.

Chargeable assets

All assets are chargeable assets unless they are specifically designated as exempt.

The following are the exempt assets that you need to be aware of:

- Motor vehicles suitable for private use
- Gilt-edged securities
- Qualifying corporate bonds (QCBs)
- Certain chattels (see later in this Text)
- Premium bonds
- Investments held in an ISA

Any gain arising on disposal of an exempt asset is not taxable and any loss is not allowable.

The exempt asset most commonly appearing in assessment questions is a car. You should not waste time computing a gain or loss on a car. All you need to do is state that the car is an exempt asset, so no gain or loss arises.

> ## Task 1
>
> Which of the following are chargeable assets for CGT purposes?
>
> (a) A diamond necklace
> (b) A cash sum invested in premium bonds that results in a substantial win
> (c) A vintage Rolls Royce

COMPUTING CHARGEABLE GAINS AND ALLOWABLE LOSSES

Whenever a chargeable asset is disposed of, a calculation to determine the amount of any gain or loss is needed. The computation follows a standard format as shown below:

	£
Disposal consideration (or market value)	100,000
Less: incidental costs of disposal	(1,000)
Net proceeds	99,000
Less: allowable costs	(28,000)
Less: enhancement expenditure	(1,000)
Chargeable gain	70,000

We will now look at each of the items in the above pro forma in turn.

Disposal consideration

Usually the disposal consideration is the proceeds of sale of the asset, but a disposal is deemed to take place at market value:

(a) Where the disposal is by way of a gift
(b) Where the disposal is made for a consideration which cannot be valued
(c) Where the disposal is made to a connected person (see below)

Costs

The following costs are deducted in the above pro forma:

(a) **Incidental costs of disposal**

These are the costs of selling an asset. They may include advertising costs, estate agents fees, legal costs or valuation fees. These costs should be deducted separately from any other allowable costs.

(b) **Allowable costs**

These include:

(i)   The original purchase price of the asset

(ii) Costs incurred in purchasing the asset (estate agents fees, legal fees etc)

(c) **Enhancement expenditure**

ENHANCEMENT EXPENDITURE is capital expenditure which enhances the value of the asset and is reflected in the state or nature of the asset at the time of disposal.

Task 2

Jack bought a holiday cottage for £25,000. He paid legal costs of £600 on the purchase.

Jack spent £8,000 building an extension to the cottage.

Jack sold the cottage for £60,000. He paid estate agent's fees of £1,200 and legal costs of £750.

Jack's gain on sale is:

£

PART DISPOSALS

Sometimes part, rather than the whole, of an asset is disposed of. For instance, one-third of a piece of land may be sold. In this case, we need to be able to compute the chargeable gain or allowable loss arising on the part of the asset disposed of.

The problem is that although we know what the disposal proceeds are for the part of the asset disposed of, we do not usually know what proportion of the cost of the whole asset relates to that part. The solution to this is to use the following fraction to determine the cost of the part disposed of.

The fraction is:

$$\frac{A}{A+B} = \frac{\text{Value of the part disposed of}}{\text{Value of the part disposed of} + \text{Market value of the remainder}}$$

A is the proceeds (or market value) before deducting incidental costs of disposal.

You must learn the above formula for use in your assessment.

The formula is used to apportion the cost of the whole asset. If, however, any expenditure was incurred wholly in respect of the part disposed of, it should be treated as an allowable deduction in full for that part and not apportioned. An example of this is incidental selling expenses, which are wholly attributable to the part disposed of.

HOW IT WORKS

Mr Jones bought four acres of land for £270,000. He sold one acre of the land at auction for £200,000, before auction expenses of 15%. The market value of the three remaining acres is £460,000.

The cost of the land being sold is:

$$\frac{200,000}{200,000 + 460,000} \times £270,000 = £81,818$$

	£
Disposal proceeds	200,000
Less: incidental costs of sale (15%)	(30,000)
Net proceeds	170,000
Less: cost (see above)	(81,818)
Chargeable gain	88,182

Task 3

Yarrek bought a plot of land for investment purposes for £100,000. In January 2010, he sold part of the land for £391,000, which was net of legal fees on the sale of £9,000. At that time, the value of the remaining land was £600,000. The chargeable gain arising on the disposal is:

£ [   ]

COMPUTING TAXABLE GAINS IN A TAX YEAR

An individual pays capital gains tax on any TAXABLE GAINS arising in a tax year.

Taxable gains are the net chargeable gains (gains minus losses) of the tax year, reduced by unrelieved losses brought forward from previous years and the annual exemption. We will look at both of these items in turn.

Annual exempt amount

All individuals are entitled to an annual exempt amount. For 2009/10 it is £10,100. It is the last deduction to be made in computing taxable gains, and effectively means that for 2009/10 the first £10,100 of chargeable gains are tax-free.

Task 4

In 2009/10 Tina has the following gains and losses:

	£
Chargeable gains	27,000
Allowable losses	9,000

Tina had no allowable losses brought forward.

Tina's taxable gains for 2009/10 are:

£ [   ]

Losses

Sometimes an allowable loss rather than a taxable gain arises. Once a loss has been calculated deal with it as follows:

(a) First, set it against gains arising in the same tax year until these are reduced to £Nil, then

(b) Set any remaining loss against net gains in the next tax year but only to reduce the net gains in the next year down to the annual exempt amount. Any loss remaining is carried forward.

HOW IT WORKS

(a) Tim has chargeable gains for 2009/10 of £25,000 and allowable losses of £16,000. As the losses are current year losses they must be fully relieved against the gains to produce net gains of £9,000, despite the fact that net gains are below the annual exempt amount.

(b) Hattie has gains of £10,600 for 2009/10 and allowable losses brought forward of £6,000. Hattie restricts her loss relief to £500 so as to leave net gains of £(10,600 – £500) = £10,100, which will be exactly covered by the annual exempt amount for 2009/10. The remaining £5,500 of losses will be carried forward to 2010/11.

(c) Mildred has chargeable gains of £2,000 for 2009/10 and losses brought forward from 2008/09 of £12,000. She will leapfrog 2009/10 and carry forward all the brought forward losses to 2010/11. The gains of £2,000 are covered by the annual exempt amount for 2009/10.

Task 5

Sally had chargeable gains of £12,000 and allowable losses of £1,000 in 2009/10. She also had allowable losses of £3,000 brought forward from 2008/09. The capital losses carried forward to 2010/11 are:

A   nil
B   £4,000
C   £1,000
D   £2,100 ✓

COMPUTING CAPITAL GAINS TAX PAYABLE

Capital gains tax is payable at the rate of 18% on an individual's taxable gains.

HOW IT WORKS

Sally made taxable gains (ie gains after deduction of the annual exemption) in 2009/10 of £20,000.

Sally's capital gains tax liability is:

£20,000 × 18%   £3,600

This is payable on 31 January 2011.

Task 6

Sarah made the following chargeable gains and allowable losses in 2009/10.

	£
Gain	21,000
Loss	4,500
Gain	17,500

The CGT payable for 2009/10 by Sarah is:

£

SELF ASSESSMENT FOR CAPITAL GAINS TAX

A taxpayer who makes chargeable gain(s) in a tax year is usually required to file details of the gain(s) in a tax return. In many cases, the taxpayer will be filing a tax return for income tax purposes and will include the capital gains supplementary pages. You will find copies of these at the end of this Chapter.

If, however, the taxpayer only has chargeable gains to report , he must notify his chargeability to HMRC by 5 October following the end of the tax year. The penalty for late notification is the same as for late notification of income tax chargeability.

The filing date for the tax return is the same as for income tax and the same penalties apply for CGT as for income tax in relation to late filing and errors on the return.

Capital gains tax is payable on 31 January following the end of the tax year. There are no payments on account. The consequences of late payment of CGT are the same as for late payment of income tax so surcharges and interest may be charged. Repayment supplement may be paid on overpayments of CGT.

CONNECTED PERSONS

If a disposal is made to a connected person the disposal is deemed to take place at the market value of the asset.

If an allowable loss arises on the disposal, it can be set only against gains arising in the same or future years from disposals to the same connected person, and the loss can only be set off if he or she is still connected with the person making the loss.

For this purpose an individual is connected with:

- His relatives (brothers, sisters, lineal ancestors and lineal descendants)
- The relatives of his spouse/civil partner
- The spouses/civil partners of his and his spouse's/civil partner's relatives

Task 7

On 1 August 2009 Holly sold a painting to her sister, Emily for £40,000. The market value of the painting on the date of sale was £50,000. Holly had bought the painting for £60,000.

What allowable loss arises on disposal of the painting and how may this be relieved?

SPOUSES/CIVIL PARTNERS

Spouses/civil partners are taxed as two separate people. Each individual has an annual exempt amount, and losses of one individual cannot be set against gains of the other.

Disposals between spouses/civil partners do not give rise to chargeable gains or allowable losses. The disposal is said to be on a 'NO GAIN/NO LOSS' basis. The acquiring spouse/civil partner takes the base cost of the disposing spouse/civil partner.

CAPITAL GAINS SUMMARY PAGES

In your assessment you may be asked to complete the capital gains summary pages.

Copies of these pages are available at the end of this chapter. You will be able to practise completing this form in the Personal Tax Question Bank.

CHAPTER OVERVIEW

- A chargeable gain arises when there is a chargeable disposal of a chargeable asset by a chargeable person

- Enhancement expenditure can be deducted in computing a chargeable gain if it is reflected in the state and nature of the asset at the time of disposal

- On the part disposal of an asset the formula A/A + B must be applied to work out the cost attributable to the part disposed of

- Taxable gains are net chargeable gains for a tax year minus losses brought forward minus the annual exempt amount

- Losses brought forward can only reduce net chargeable gains down to the amount of the annual exempt amount

- CGT is payable at 18% by 31 January following the end of the tax year

- CGT Is self assessed and has the same rules about notification of chargeability, penalties and interest as income tax

- A disposal to a connected person takes place at market value

- For individuals, connected people are broadly brothers, sisters, lineal ancestors and descendants and their spouses/civil partners plus similar relations of a spouse/civil partner

- Losses on disposals to connected people can only be set against gains on disposals to the same connected person

- Disposals between spouses/civil partners take place on a no gain/no loss basis

Keywords

Chargeable person – an individual

Chargeable asset – any asset that is not an exempt asset

Chargeable disposal – a sale or gift of an asset

Exempt disposal – a disposal on which no chargeable gain or allowable loss arises

Enhancement expenditure – capital expenditure that enhances the value of the asset and is reflected in the state or nature of the asset at the time of disposal

Taxable gains – the net chargeable gains of a tax year, after deducting losses and the annual exempt amount

No gain/no loss disposal –a disposal on which no gain or loss arises

TEST YOUR LEARNING

Test 1

Which of the following constitute chargeable disposals for CGT?

(a)   A gift of an antique necklace

(b)   The sale of a building?

Test 2

Yvette buys an investment property for £325,000. She sells the property on 12 December 2009 for £560,000. Her gain on sale is:

£

Test 3

Richard sells four acres of land (out of a plot of ten acres) for £38,000 in May 2009. Costs of disposal amount to £3,000. The ten-acre plot cost £41,500. The market value of the six acres remaining is £48,000.

The chargeable gain/allowable loss arising is:

A   £16,663

B   £18,400

C   £19,663

D   £18,337

$$\frac{38,000}{38,000 + 48,000} \times 41,500$$

18337

Test 4

Philip has chargeable gains of £171,000 and allowable losses of £5,300 in 2009/10. Losses brought forward at 6 April 2009 amount to £10,000. What amount is liable to CGT in 2009/10? What are the losses carried forward?

£

$$\begin{array}{r} 171,000 \\ 5,300 \\ \hline 165,700 \\ -10,000 \end{array}$$

Test 5

Martha's CGT liability for 2009/10, assuming she has chargeable gains (before the annual exempt amount) of £23,800 is:

£

Test 6

True/False. A loss arising on a disposal to a connected person can be set against any gains arising in the same year or in subsequent years.

Test 7

True/False. No gain or loss arises on a disposal to a spouse/civil partner.

Capital gains summary

Tax year 6 April 2009 to 5 April 2010

| 1 | Your name | | 2 | Your unique taxpayer reference (UTR) |

Summary of your enclosed computations

You **must** enclose your computations, as well as filling in the boxes – read page CGN 9 of the *notes*.

3	Total gains in the year, before losses
£ · 0 0

4	Total losses of the year – *enter '0' if there are none*
£ · 0 0

5	Losses brought forward and used in the year
£ · 0 0

6	Total gains, after losses but before the annual exempt amount
£ · 0 0

7	Annual exempt amount
£ · 0 0

8	Net chargeable gains (box 6 minus box 7) – *but if box 7 is more than box 6, leave blank*
£ · 0 0

9	Additional liability in respect of non-resident or dual resident trusts
£ · 0 0

10	Losses available to be carried forward to later years
£ · 0 0

11	Losses used against an earlier year's gain (special circumstances apply – *read the notes on page CGN 11*)
£ · 0 0

12	Losses used against income – *amount claimed against 2009–10 income*
£ · 0 0

13	Losses used against income – *amount claimed against 2008–09 income*
£ · 0 0

14	Income losses of 2009–10 set against gains
£ · 0 0

15	Entrepreneurs' relief – *read the notes on pages CGN 7 and CGN 8*
£ · 0 0

Listed shares and securities

16	Number of disposals

17	Disposal proceeds
£ · 0 0

18	Allowable costs (including purchase price)
£ · 0 0

19	Gains in the year, before losses
£ · 0 0

20	If you are making any claim or election, put 'X' in the box

21	If your computations include any estimates or valuations, put 'X' in the box

Unlisted shares and securities

22	Number of disposals

23	Disposal proceeds
£	. 0 0

24	Allowable costs (including purchase price)
£	. 0 0

25	Gains in the year, before losses
£	. 0 0

26	If you are making any claim or election, put 'X' in the box

27	If your computations include any estimates or valuations, put 'X' in the box

Property and other assets and gains

28	Number of disposals

29	Disposal proceeds
£	. 0 0

30	Allowable costs (including purchase price)
£	. 0 0

31	Gains in the year, before losses
£	. 0 0

32	Attributed gains where personal losses cannot be set-off
£	. 0 0

33	If you are making any claim or election, put 'X' in the box

34	If your computations include any estimates or valuations, put 'X' in the box

Any other information

35	Please give any other information in this space

chapter 8:
CHATTELS AND PRIVATE RESIDENCES

chapter coverage 📖

In this chapter we see how to compute gains and losses arising on the disposal of chattels. We look at the exemption that is available for any gain that arises on the disposal of an individual's private residence.

The topics covered are:

✎   Chattels

✎   Private residences

CHATTELS

A CHATTEL is tangible moveable property (ie property that can be moved, seen and touched). Examples are items such as furniture and works of art.

A WASTING CHATTEL is a chattel with an estimated remaining useful life of 50 years or less. An example would be a racehorse or a greyhound. Wasting chattels are exempt from CGT (so that there are no chargeable gains and no allowable losses). There is one exception to this, but this is not assessable in your assessment.

Task 1

Jamiel bought a racing greyhound for £6,000. The greyhound was sold for £10,000.

True/False: a chargeable gain of £4,000 arises on the disposal.

There are special rules for calculating gains and losses on non-wasting chattels:

(a) If a chattel is not a wasting asset, any gain arising on its disposal will still be exempt from CGT if the asset is sold for gross proceeds of £6,000 or less

(b) If sale proceeds exceed £6,000, but the cost is less than £6,000 the gain is limited to:

5/3 × (gross proceeds – £6,000)

(c) If sale proceeds are less than £6,000, any allowable loss is restricted to that which would arise if it were sold for gross proceeds of £6,000

We will have a look at examples of each of these situations in turn.

HOW IT WORKS

An individual art collector purchased a painting for £3,000. On 1 January 2010 he sold the painting at auction.

If the gross sale proceeds are £4,000, the gain on sale will be exempt.

If the gross proceeds are £8,000 with costs of sale of 10%, the gain arising on the disposal of the painting will be calculated as follows:

	£
Gross proceeds	8,000
Less: incidental costs of sale (10%)	(800)
Net proceeds	7,200
Less: cost	(3,000)
Chargeable gain	4,200
Gain cannot exceed 5/3 × £(8,000 − 6,000)	£3,333

Task 2

Jacky purchased a non-wasting chattel for £2,500. On 1 October 2009 she sold the chattel at auction for £9,500 (which was after deducting the auctioneer's 5% commission). The gain arising is:

A   nil
B   £5,833
C   £7,500
D   £6,667 ✓

HOW IT WORKS

Magee purchased an antique desk for £8,000. She sold the desk in an auction for £4,750 net of auctioneer's fees of 5%.

Magee obviously has a loss and therefore the allowable loss is calculated on deemed proceeds of £6,000. The costs of disposal can be deducted from the deemed proceeds of £6,000.

	£
Deemed disposal proceeds	6,000
Less: incidental costs of disposal (£4,750 × 5/95)	(250)
	5,750
Less: cost	(8,000)
Allowable loss	(2,250)

Task 3

Jameel purchased a non-wasting chattel for £8,800 which he sold at auction for £3,600 (which was net of 10% commission). The allowable loss is:

£ (3,200)

HOW IT WORKS

Miguel owned three vases. He had bought these together for £7,500. He sold one of the vases in October 2009 for £9,000. The other two vases were worth £13,500 at that time.

The gain on sale of one vase

	£
Proceeds	9,000
Less: cost (9/(9 + 13.5)) × £7,500	(3,000)
Gain	6,000
Gain cannot exceed 5/3 x £(9,000 – 6,000)	5,000

Note. There are special rules that prevent taxpayers splitting up a set of assets and selling them separately in order to use the £6,000 exemption, but these rules are not in your syllabus.

Task 4

In 2009/10, Mr California sold the following chattels.

Chattel	Cost	Proceeds
	£	£
Vase	800	7,000
Sideboard	7,000	5,000

All proceeds are shown before selling expenses of 5% of the gross proceeds. Compute the chargeable gain or allowable loss on each chattel.

1667

-1250

PRIVATE RESIDENCES

A gain arising on the sale of an individual's only or main private residence (PRINCIPAL PRIVATE RESIDENCE) is exempt from CGT. Any loss is not allowable.

Spouses/civil partners are entitled to only one principal private residence between them. This applies even though they are generally taxed independently.

The basic rule is that the gain is wholly exempt where the owner has occupied the whole of the residence throughout his period of ownership. Where occupation has been for only part of the period, the proportion of the gain exempted is:

$$\text{Total gain} \times \frac{\text{Period of occupation}}{\text{Total period of ownership}}$$

The last 36 months of ownership is exempt in all cases if, at some time, the residence has been the taxpayer's main residence.

Task 5

Clare bought herself a flat in April 2004 for £80,000. She lived in the flat until March 2007 when she moved to a farmhouse she had bought to be her main residence. The flat was empty until it was sold in March 2010 for £300,000.

True/False: the gain arising on the sale is completely exempt.

Deemed occupation

The period of occupation is also deemed to include certain periods of absence, provided the individual had no other main residence at that time and the period of absence was at some time both preceded by and followed by a period of actual occupation.

These periods of DEEMED OCCUPATION are:

(a) Any period (or periods taken together) of absence, for any reason, not exceeding three years. Where such a period exceeds three years, three years out of the longer period are deemed to be a period of occupation;

(b) Any periods during which the owner was required by his employment to live abroad;

(c) Any period (or periods taken together) not exceeding four years where the owner was:

   (i) Self-employed and forced to work away from home (UK and abroad); or

   (ii) Employed and required to work elsewhere in the UK (overseas employment is covered by (b) above).

A period of absence may be treated as deemed occupation under the above rules, even if the residence is let while the owner is away.

HOW IT WORKS

Mr A purchased a house for £50,000 on 31 March 1990. He lived in the house until 30 June 1990. He was then sent to work abroad by his employer for five years before returning to the UK to live in the house again on 1 July 1995. He stayed in the house for six months before moving out to live with friends until the house was sold on 31 December 2009 for £150,000.

First work out what periods are chargeable and which are exempt:

		Exempt months	Chargeable months
(i)	1 April 1990 to 30 June 1990	3	–
(ii)	1 July 1990 to 30 June 1995	60	–
(iii)	1 July 1995 to 31 December 1995	6	–
(iv)	1 January 1996 to 31 December 2006	–	132
(v)	1 January 2007 to 31 December 2009	36	–
		105	132

Explanations:

(i) *April 1990 to June 1990.* Actual occupation.

(ii) *July 1990 to June 1995.* Covered by the exemption for periods of absence during which the owner is required by his employment to live abroad. The period is both preceded and followed by a period of owner occupation.

(iii) *July 1995 to December 1995.* Actual occupation.

(iv) *January 1996 to December 2006.* This period is not eligible to be partly covered by the exemption for three years of absence for any reason, as it is not followed by a period of actual occupation.

(v) *January 2007 to December 2009.* Covered by the final 36 months exemption.

Then calculate the chargeable gain after the exemption has been applied:

	£
Disposal proceeds	150,000
Less: cost	(50,000)
	100,000

Less: exempt under PPR provisions

$$\frac{105}{105 + 132} \times £100,000$$

	(44,304)
Chargeable gain	55,696

In this example, had Mr A gone straight to live with friends in July 1995 instead of having six months occupation, he would have lost not only the extra six months, but also the period from July 1990 to June 1995, as this period of absence would lose its status of deemed occupation as the property was not occupied again by the owner prior to sale.

Task 6

Shammima bought a house on 1 May 2003 for £80,000. She lived in the house until
30 April 2004 when she went to stay with her elderly mother for two years. Shammima returned to the house on 1 May 2006 and lived in it until 31 August 2006. She went to live in a new house she had bought on 1 September 2006. The first house was sold on 28 February 2010 for £200,000. Calculate the gain arising on disposal of the first house.

CHAPTER OVERVIEW

- Wasting chattels are exempt assets for CGT purposes (eg racehorses and greyhounds)

- Non-wasting chattels are exempt if they are sold for gross proceeds of £6,000 or less. If gross proceeds exceed £6,000 any gain arising on the disposal of the asset is limited to 5/3 (Gross proceeds − £6,000)

- If the gross proceeds are less than £6,000 on the sale of a non-wasting chattel, any loss otherwise arising is restricted by deeming the gross proceeds to be £6,000

- Any gain arising on the disposal of an individual's principal private residence is exempt from CGT. A loss is not allowable

- Certain periods of non-occupation count as periods of deemed occupation

- The last 36 months of ownership always count as a period of occupation

Keywords

Chattel – tangible moveable property

Wasting chattel – a chattel with an estimated remaining useful life of 50 years or less

Principal private residence – an individual's only or main residence

Deemed occupation – periods during which an individual is treated as having occupied a residence

TEST YOUR LEARNING

Test 1

Mustafa bought a non-wasting chattel for £3,500. Compute the gain arising if he sells it for:

(a) £5,800 after deducting selling expenses of £180 — No gain below 6,000?

(b) £8,200 after deducting selling expenses of £220 — 4,033 ✓

Test 2

Simon bought a racehorse for £4,500. He sold the racehorse for £9,000. The gain arising is:

£ NIL

Test 3

Santa bought a painting for £7,000. He sold the painting in June 2009 for £5,000. The loss arising is:

£ (1000)

Test 4

Provided the property has at some time been the owner's principal private residence, the last .... months of ownership is always an exempt period. How many months?

A   12

B   24

C   36

D   48

Test 5

Give three examples of periods of absence from a property which are deemed periods of occupation for the CGT principal private residence exemption.

Test 6

Josephine purchased a house on 1 April 1992 for £60,000 and used it as her main residence until 10 August 1995 when she was sent by her employer to manage the Paris office. She worked and lived in Paris until 9 August 1999. Josephine returned to live in the house on 10 August 1999 but moved out to live in a new house (to be treated as her main residence) on 2 May 2001. The property was sold on 30 November 2009 for £180,000. Compute the gain on sale.

chapter 9:
SHARES

chapter coverage 📖

In this chapter we see how to compute chargeable gains and allowable losses on the disposal of shares.

This is a very important chapter as the computation of gains and losses on the disposal of shares is a key task in your assessment. Shares may be assessed as a long question, so you need to be prepared to set out a computation in the way outlined in this chapter.

The topics covered are:

✍ Why special rules are needed for shares

✍ Matching rules

✍ Share pool

✍ Bonus and rights issues

✍ Listed and unlisted shares

WHY SPECIAL RULES ARE NEEDED FOR SHARES

Shares present special problems when computing gains or losses on disposal. For instance, suppose that a taxpayer buys some shares in X plc on the following dates:

	No of shares	Cost
		£
5 July 1991	100	150
17 January 1996	100	375
2 July 2009	100	1,000

On 15 June 2009, he sells 220 of his shares for £3,300. To work out his chargeable gain, we need to be able to identify which shares out of his three holdings were actually sold. Since one share is identical to any other, it is not possible to work this out by reference to factual evidence.

As a result, it has been necessary to devise 'matching rules'. These allow HMRC to identify on a disposal which shares have been sold and so work out what the allowable cost (and therefore the gain) on disposal should be. These matching rules are considered in detail below.

It is very important that you understand the matching rules. These rules are very regularly assessed and if you do not understand them you will not be able to get any of this part of a task right.

MATCHING RULES

For individuals the matching of the shares sold is in the following order:

    (a)   Shares acquired on the same day

    (b)   Shares acquired in the following thirty days on a FIFO (first in, first out) basis

    (c)   Shares from the share pool

SHARE POOL

The share pool includes shares acquired up to the day before the disposal on which we are calculating the gain or loss. It grows when an acquisition is made and shrinks when a disposal is made.

The calculation of the share pool value

To compute the value of the share pool, set-up two columns of figures:

(a) The number of shares
(b) The cost of the shares

HOW IT WORKS

Jackie bought 10,000 shares in X plc for £6,000 in August 1992 and another 10,000 shares for £9,000 in December 2004.

She sold 12,000 shares for £24,000 in August 2009.

The share pool is:

	No of shares	Cost £
8.92 Acquisition	10,000	6,000
12.04 Acquisition	10,000	9,000
	20,000	15,000
8.09 Disposal	(12,000)	(9,000)
c/f	8,000	6,000

The gain is:

	£
Proceeds of sale	24,000
Less: allowable cost	(9,000)
Chargeable gain	15,000

Task 1

Joraver bought 9,000 shares in Z plc for £4,500 in May 1996. He sold 2,000 shares in August 2005. He then bought a further 5,000 shares for £7,500 in May 2008.

Joraver sold 10,000 shares for £20,000 in January 2010.

The gain on the sale in 2010 is:

£ 10833

HOW IT WORKS

Tony bought shares in A Ltd as follows.

11 May 2001	10,000 shares for £20,000
9 April 2006	5,000 shares for £12,000
15 June 2009	5,000 shares for £15,000

He sold 18,000 shares for £49,500 on 5 June 2009.

The disposal is matched first against the acquisition in the next 30 days as follows.

	£
Proceeds of sale $\frac{5,000}{18,000} \times £49,500$	13,750
Less: allowable cost	(15,000)
Allowable loss	(1,250)

Then the disposal is matched against the share pool.

	£
Proceeds of sale $\frac{13,000}{18,000} \times £49,500$	35,750
Less: allowable cost (W)	(27,733)
Chargeable gain	8,017

Therefore the net chargeable gain is:

£(8,017 – 1,250)	6,767

Working	No of shares	Cost
		£
11.5.01 Acquisition	10,000	20,000
9.4.06 Acquisition	5,000	12,000
	15,000	32,000
5.6.09 Disposal	(13,000)	(27,733)
c/f	2,000	4,267

Task 2

Eliot acquired shares in K Ltd as follows.

10 August 2003	5,000 shares for £10,000
15 April 2006	2,000 shares for £5,000
25 July 2009	1,000 shares for £3,800
27 July 2009	500 shares for £1,700

Eliot sold 6,000 shares for £21,600 on 25 July 2009.

Calculate the net chargeable gain arising on the disposal by Eliot.

BONUS AND RIGHTS ISSUES

Bonus issues

BONUS SHARES are additional shares given free to shareholders based on their current holding(s). For example, a shareholder may own 2,000 shares. The company makes a 1 share for every 2 shares held bonus issue (called 1 for 2 bonus issue). The shareholder will then have an extra 1,000 shares, giving him 3,000 shares overall.

Bonus shares are treated as being acquired at the date of the original acquisition of the underlying shares giving rise to the bonus issue.

Since bonus shares are issued at no cost there is no need to adjust the original cost.

Rights issues

In a RIGHTS ISSUE, a shareholder is offered additional shares by the company in proportion to the shares he already holds.

The difference between a bonus issue and a rights issue is that in a rights issue the new shares are paid for. This results in an adjustment to the original cost.

If the shareholder decides not to take up the rights issue shares, there is usually no effect for CGT.

HOW IT WORKS

Jonah acquired 20,000 shares for £36,000 in T plc in April 2001. There was a 1 for 2 bonus issue in May 2006 and a 1 for 5 rights issue in August 2009 at £1.20 per share.

Jonah sold 30,000 shares for £45,000 in December 2009.

The share pool is constructed as follows:

	No of shares	Cost
		£
4.01 Acquisition	20,000	36,000
5.06 Bonus 1 for 2	10,000	–
	30,000	36,000
8.09 Rights 1 for 5 @ £1.20	6,000	7,200
	36,000	43,200
12.09 Disposal	(30,000)	(36,000)
c/f	6,000	7,200

The gain on sale is:

	£
Proceeds of sale	45,000
Less: allowable cost	(36,000)
Chargeable gain	9,000

Task 3

Dorothy bought 2,000 shares for £10,000 in S Ltd in August 2001. There was a 1 for 1 rights issue at £2.50 in May 2004 and Dorothy took up all her rights issue shares. There was a 1 for 4 bonus issue in September 2007.

Dorothy sold 3,000 shares for £18,000 in October 2009.

Her chargeable gain on sale is:

£	6000

LISTED AND UNLISTED SHARES

The capital gains summary pages require you to show gains on listed and unlisted shares separately. There is no difference in the computation of gains.

LISTED SHARES are listed on a Stock Exchange. A listed company will always have the letters plc (public limited company) in its name.

UNLISTED SHARES are not listed on a Stock Exchange. An unlisted company will have either Ltd (Limited) or plc (public limited company) in its name.

You should be told in the assessment whether shares are listed or unlisted if relevant.

CHAPTER OVERVIEW

- The matching rules for individuals are:
    - Same day acquisitions
    - Next 30 days acquisitions on a FIFO basis
    - Shares in the share pool
- The share pool runs up to the day before disposal
- Bonus issue and rights issue shares are acquired in proportion to the shareholder's existing holding
- The difference between a bonus and a rights issue is that in a rights issue shares are paid for
- Listed shares are listed on a Stock Exchange, unlisted shares are not listed on a Stock Exchange

Keywords

Bonus shares – shares that are issued free to shareholders based on original holdings

Rights issues – similar to bonus issues except that in a rights issue shares must be paid for

Listed shares – shares listed on a Stock Exchange

Unlisted shares – shares not listed on a Stock Exchange

£

2000	10,000
2000	5,000
4000	15,000
1000	

18000
9000
6,000 GAIN

5000
(3000)
2000

15000
(9000)
6000

TEST YOUR LEARNING

Test 1

Tasha bought 10,000 shares in V plc in August 1991 for £5,000 and a further 10,000 shares for £16,000 in April 2006. She sold 15,000 shares for £30,000 in November 2009.

Her chargeable gain is:

A   £9,000
B   £11,500
C   £17,000
D   £14,250

(handwritten working)

£
10,000   5,000
10,000   16,000
20,000   21,000
(15000) (15,750)

Test 2

True/False: in both a bonus issue and a rights issue, there is an adjustment to the original cost of the shares.

Test 3

Marcus bought 2,000 shares in X plc in May 2000 for £12,000. There was a 1 for 2 rights issue at £7.50 per share in December 2001. Marcus sold 2,500 shares for £20,000 in March 2010. His chargeable gain is:

£ | 3750

(handwritten working)

2000   12,000
1000   7,500
3000   19,500
(2500) (16,250)
500   3,250

ANSWERS TO CHAPTER TASKS

Chapter 1:   The tax framework

1   31 January 2016

2   You should tell Cornelius that under the AAT *Guidelines* on client confidentiality, you cannot provide him with any information on another client without the specific authority of that client.

Chapter 2:   Employment income

1   £(20,000 + 5,000) = £25,000.

The bonus is received when Rio becomes entitled to it. It is not linked to period during which it was earned (the company's period of account).

2   C

10 April 2010 as this is the date when the amount is determined (after the date the company's accounting period ends).

3   The CO_2 emissions of the car are 215g/km (rounded down to the nearest five below)

Amount over baseline figure 215 – 135 = 80g/ km

Divide by 5 = 16

The taxable percentage is 15% + 16% = 31%

So the benefit is 31% × £10,000 × 9/12 =   £2,325

Note. The benefit is multiplied by 9/12 as the car was only available for nine months in the tax year.

4   D

Round down CO_2 emissions to 190 g/km

Amount above baseline: 190 – 135 = 55 g/km

Divide by 5 = 11

Taxable % = 15% + 11% + 3% (diesel) = 29%

	£
Car benefit £30,000 × 29%	8,700
Fuel benefit £16,900 × 29%	4,901
Total benefit	13,601

Note. No deduction is made in respect of the amount paid towards the cost of private fuel.

5 *2008/09*

Use benefit £6,000 × 20% = £1,200

2009/10

Use benefit £6,000 × 20% × 3/12 = £300

Acquisition	£	£
(i) Market value at acquisition	4,000	–
(ii) Market value when first provided	–	6,000
Less: assessed in respect of use £(1,200 + 300)	–	(1,500)
	4,000	4,500
Less: amount paid	(1,000)	(1,000)
	3,000	3,500

Take higher, £3,500

6 $\dfrac{£6,200 + £5,200}{2} \times 4.75\% = £271$

As no elections are made, the 'average' method of valuing the loan is used.

7 Interest: no benefit because loan not over £5,000.

Loan written-off: £4,000 × 35% = £1,400 taxable benefit.

8 A

	£
Annual value	5,200
Additional benefit £(600,000 – 75,000) × 4.75%	24,938
	30,138
Less: rent paid	(12,000)
Taxable benefit	18,138

9		£	£
Salary (= net earnings)			27,400
Accommodation benefits			
Annual value: exempt (job-related)			
Ancillary services			
Electricity		550	
Gas		400	
Gardener		750	
Redecoration		1,800	
		3,500	
Restricted to 10% of £27,400		2,740	
Less employee's contribution (12 × £50)		(600)	
			2,140
Employment income			29,540

10		£	£
Amount received 12,000 × 38p			4,560
Less: statutory limit			
10,000 × 40p		4,000	
2,000 × 25p		500	
			(4,500)
Taxable benefit			60

11		£
Mileage allowance received (12,000 × 25p)		3,000
Less: statutory allowance		
(10,000 × 40p) + (2,000 × 25p)		(4,500)
Excess of statutory allowance		(1,500)

£3,000 is tax-free. Tax relief can be claimed on £1,500, the excess of the statutory allowance over the amount received.

Chapter 3:   Property income

1		£	£
Rental income (£160 × 10)			1,600
Rental income (£400 × 1)			400
Less: bad debt		300	
interest		700	
			(1,000)
Taxable property income			1,000

2		£	£
Rental income: property 1(accrued)			14,000
property 2 (3/12 × £6,800)			1,700
Less: agent's fees			
(15% × £(14,000 + 1,700))		2,355	
insurance on Whitehouse			
(3/12 × £1,200 + 9/12 × £1,400)		1,350	
insurance on Blackhouse			
(3/12 × £980 + 9/12 × £1,100)		1,070	
advertising for tenants		450	
			(5,225)
Taxable property income			10,475

3   A

		£	£
Rental income			12,000
Less: water rates		800	
council tax		900	
agents fees		1,200	
wear and tear allowance			
10% × £(12,000 – 800 – 900)		1,030	
			(3,930)
Taxable property income			8,070

4   Jordan and Merry each receive rental income of £(80 × 52)/2 = £2,080. They each have a rent-a-room limit of £2,125. Since the rental is less than the limit, the rent is wholly exempt from income tax for them. The expenses are ignored. It is possible to elect to ignore rent-a-room relief but this will not be beneficial in this case.

Chapter 4: Taxable income

1   £160 × 100/80 = £200

2   Dividends   £900 × 100/90   = £1,000

Interest   £1,600 × 100/80   = £2,000

3   C

NatWest deposit a/c interest

£80 × 100/80   £100

Dividend income on an ISA and interest on the maturity of NS&I savings certificates are exempt from income tax.

4

	Non-savings income	Savings income	Dividend income	Total
	£	£	£	£
Business income	44,000			
Building society interest		2,000		
Dividends			1,000	
Total income	44,000	2,000	1,000	47,000

Lotto winnings are exempt from income tax.

5

	Non-savings Income	Savings income	Dividend income	Total
	£	£	£	£
Trade profits	10,000			
Bank interest (× 100/80)		2,500		
Dividends (× 100/90)			5,000	
Total income	10,000	2,500	5,000	17,500
Less: personal allowance	(6,475)			
Taxable income	3,525	2,500	5,000	11,025

Premium bond prizes are exempt from income tax.

6

	Non-savings Income	Savings income	Dividend income	Total
	£	£	£	£
Pension income	17,500			
Bank interest (× 100/80)		2,500		
Dividends (× 100/90)			5,000	
Total income	17,500	2,500	5,000	25,000

	£
Total income	25,000
Less: income limit	(22,900)
Excess	2,100
Age allowance	9,640
Less: half excess	(1,050)
Amount available	8,590

7

	£
Total income	29,000
Less: Gift Aid donation	(500)
Adjusted total income	28,500
Less: income limit	(22,900)
Excess	5,600
Age allowance	9,640
Less: half excess	(2,800)
Adjusted age allowance	6,840

Chapter 5: Calculation of income tax

1

	Non-savings income	Savings income	Total
	£	£	£
Taxable income	25,000	35,000	60,000

Tax on non-savings income

£25,000 × 20%   5,000

Tax on savings income

(£37,400 − £25,000) = £12,400

× 20%   2,480

£22,600 × 40%   9,040

35,000   Tax liability 16,520

2

	Non-savings income	Savings income	Total
	£	£	£
Employment income	7,000		
Bank interest (£4,000 × 100/80)		5,000	
Net income	7,000	5,000	12,000
Less: personal allowance	(6,475)		
Taxable income	525	5,000	5,525

Tax on non-savings income

£525 × 20%   105.00

Tax on savings income

£(2,440 − 525) = 1,915 × 10%   191.50

£(5,000 − 1,915) = 3,085 × 20%   617.00

Income tax liability   913.50

3 D

	Non-savings income	Savings income	Total
	£	£	£
Taxable income	24,000	26,000	50,000

Tax on non-savings income

£24,000 × 20%	4,800.00

Tax on savings income

£13,400 (£37,400 − £24,000) × 20%	2,680.00
£7,000 (£5,600 × 100/80) × 20%	1,400.00
£5,600 × 40%	2,240.00
26,000	11,120.00

Note. The basic rate band is extended by the gross amount of the personal pension contribution paid.

4

	Dividend income
	£
Dividends (× 100/90)	25,000
Less: personal allowance	(6,475)
Taxable income	18,525

Tax on dividend income	£
£18,525 × 10%	1,852.50
Less: tax credit on dividend (max)	(1,852.50)
Tax payable	nil

5

	Non-savings income £	Savings income £	Dividend income £	Total £
Rental income	31,000			
Bank interest (× 100/80)		10,000		
Dividends (× 100/90)			12,000	
Total income	31,000	10,000	12,000	53,000
Less: personal allowance	(6,475)			
Taxable income	24,525	10,000	12,000	46,525

	£
Tax on non-savings income	
£24,525 × 20%	4,905.00
Tax on savings income	
£10,000 × 20%	2,000.00
Tax on dividend income	
£2,875 £(37,400 − 24,525 − 10,000) × 10%	287.50
£9,125 × 32.5%	2,965.62
12,000	10,158.12
Less: tax credit on dividend	(1,200.00)
tax suffered on interest	(2,000.00)
Income tax payable	6,958.12

6

	Non-savings income £	Savings income £	Total £
Employment income	14,955		
Building society interest (× 100/80)		5,000	
Total income	14,955	5,000	19,955
Less: personal allowance	(9,490)		
Taxable income	5,465	5,000	10,465

	£
Tax on non-savings income	
£5,465 × 20%	1,093.00
Tax on savings income	
£5,000 × 20%	1,000.00
Tax liability	2,093.00
Less: tax deducted from employment income	(900.00)
tax suffered on building society interest	(1,000.00)
Tax payable	193.00

Note that both tax suffered on building society interest and tax suffered on employment income are deducted from the tax liability to arrive at tax payable. If these amounts had exceeded the tax liability, the excess could have been repaid.

Chapter 6:   Self-assessment of income tax

1   Since the notice to file was issued after 31 October 2010, the filing date is three months after the notice was issued, ie 2 February 2011.

2   Payments on account $\dfrac{£14,000}{2} = £7,000$

No payments on account are due in respect of CGT.

Chapter 7:   Computing capital gains tax

1   The diamond necklace only. The other assets are exempt assets.

2

	£
Proceeds of sale	60,000
Less: costs of disposal £(1,200 + 750)	(1,950)
Net proceeds of sale	58,050
Less: original cost	(25,000)
costs of acquisition	(600)
enhancement expenditure	(8,000)
Chargeable gain	24,450

3

	£
Proceeds	400,000
Less: costs of disposal	(9,000)
Net proceeds of sale	391,000
Less: cost	
(400,000/400,000 + 600,000) x £100,000	(40,000)
Chargeable gain	351,000

4

	£
Chargeable gains	27,000
Less: allowable losses	(9,000)
	18,000
Less: annual exempt amount	(10,100)
Taxable gains	7,900

5 D

	£
Chargeable gains	12,000
Less: allowable losses	(1,000)
	11,000
Less: capital losses b/f	(900)
Net gain	10,100

Losses c/f £2,100 £(3,000 – 900)

6

	£
Gain	21,000
Gain	17,500
Loss	(4,500)
Net chargeable gains	34,000
Less: annual exempt amount	(10,100)
Taxable gains	23,900
CGT @ 18% on £23,900	4,302

7

	£
Deemed proceeds (market value)	50,000
Less: cost	(60,000)
Allowable loss	(10,000)

The loss may only be set against gains arising on the disposal of other assets by Holly to Emily.

Chapter 8: Chattels and private residences

1 False. No chargeable gain/allowable loss arises as greyhounds are exempt assets as they are wasting chattels.

2 D

	£
Proceeds	10,000
Less: commission (5%)	(500)
	9,500
Less: cost	(2,500)
	7,000

Maximum gain 5/3 × £(10,000 – 6,000) = £6,667

Therefore, gain = £6,667

3

	£
Deemed proceeds	6,000
Less: commission (£3,600 × 10/90)	(400)
	5,600
Less: cost	(8,800)
Allowable loss	(3,200)

4 (a) *The vase*

	£
Proceeds	7,000
Less: selling expenses	(350)
	6,650
Less: cost	(800)
Gain	5,850

The gain is the lower of £5,850 and £(7,000 – 6,000) × 5/3 = £1,667, so it is £1,667.

(b) *The sideboard*   £
    Proceeds (deemed)   6,000
    Less: selling expenses (5,000 × 5%)   (250)
                                                 5,750

    Less: cost   (7,000)
    Loss   (1,250)

5   True. The gain arising on the disposal of the flat is completely exempt.

    Clare was in actual occupation from April 2004 to March 2007.

    The last 36 months of ownership are exempt because Clare had previously lived in the flat as her only or main residence.

6

	Actual or deemed occupation months	*Non-occupation months*
1 May 2003 to 30 April 2004	12	
1 May 2004 to 30 April 2006	24	
(2 years any reason)		
1 May 2006 to 31 August 2006	4	
1 September 2006 to 28 February 2007		6
1 March 2007 to 28 February 2010	36	—
	76	6

	£
Sale proceeds	200,000
Less: cost	(80,000)
	120,000
Less: £120,000 × 76/82	(111,220)
Chargeable gain	8,780

Chapter 9: Shares

1   Share pool

	No of shares	Cost
		£
5.96 Acquisition	9,000	4,500
8.05 Disposal	(2,000)	(1,000)
c/f	7,000	3,500
5.08 Acquisition	5,000	7,500
	12,000	11,000
1.10 Disposal	(10,000)	(9,167)
c/f	2,000	1,833

Gain£		
Proceeds of sale		20,000
Less: cost		(9,167)
Chargeable gain		10,833

2   Match the disposal first with the same day acquisition:

	£
Proceeds of sale $\dfrac{1,000}{6,000} \times £21,600$	3,600
Less: cost	(3,800)
Allowable loss	(200)

Then match with the acquisition in the next 30 days:

	£
Proceeds of sale $\dfrac{500}{6,000} \times £21,600$	1,800
Less: allowable cost	(1,700)
Chargeable gain	100 ✓

Finally, match with the share pool:

	£
Proceeds of sale $\dfrac{4,500}{6,000} \times £21,600$	16,200
Less: allowable cost (W)	(9,643)
Chargeable gain	6,557

The net chargeable gain is therefore:
£(100 + 6,557 – 200)   £6,457

Working

	No of shares	Cost
		£
10.8.03 Acquisition	5,000	10,000
15.4.06 Acquisition	2,000	5,000
	7,000	15,000
25.7.09 Disposal	(4,500)	(9,643)
c/f	2,500	5,357

3

	£
Proceeds of sale	18,000
Less: allowable cost (W)	(9,000)
Chargeable gain	9,000

Working

Share pool	No of shares	Cost
		£
8.01 Acquisition	2,000	10,000
5.04 Rights issue 1 for 1 @ £2.50	2,000	5,000
c/f	4,000	15,000
9.07 Bonus 1 for 4	1,000	–
	5,000	15,000
10.09 Disposal	(3,000)	(9,000)
c/f	2,000	6,000

Answers to chapter tasks

TEST YOUR LEARNING – ANSWERS

Chapter 1: The tax framework

1   False.

    Most taxpayers have all their tax deducted at source and are not sent a tax return.

2   Statute law and case law

3   B

    When discussing client affairs with third parties with the client's proper and specific authority

4   C

    Serious Organised Crime Authority

Chapter 2: Employment income

1   Self-employed: contract **for services**

    Employee: contract **of service**

2   **Wholly, exclusively** and **necessarily**.

3

	£
Amount received 8,000 × 35p	2,800
Less: 8,000 × 40p	(3,200)
Deductible amount	(400)

    £400 is deductible in computing employment income.

4   £3,900, being the higher of the annual value and rent actually paid by the employer

5   False. There is a taxable fuel benefit unless the employer is fully reimbursed for private fuel.

6 D

Benefit is based on the highest of:

	£	£
(a) Current MV		325
(b) Original MV	500	
Less: already assessed (in 2008/09)		
£500 × 20%	(100)	
	400	

ie £400

Therefore the taxable benefit after deduction of the amount paid (£150) is £250.

7 False. Only if the loan does not exceed £5,000 at any time in the tax year is it ignored.

8 CO_2 emissions = 180 g/km (rounded down)

Above baseline 180 – 135 = 45 g/km

Divide by 5 = 45/5 = 9

Percentage = 15% + 9% = 24%

Benefit 24% × £24,000 = £5,760

9

	£
Car benefit (W)	19,440
Fuel benefit (£16,900 × 27%)	4,563
Telephone benefit (exempt – one mobile phone)	NIL
Total benefit	24,003

Working

Amount of emissions above baseline 195 – 135 = 60 g/km

Divide by 5 = 12

Percentage = 15% + 12% = 27%

£72,000 × 27% = £19,440

Chapter 3: Property income

1 Rental income 2009/10:

Rent accrued 1 December 2009 to 5 April 2010, ie $4/12 \times £3,600 = £1,200$.

2 B

Wear and tear allowance against rents:

$10\% \times £(16,000 - 320 - 780) = £1,490$

3 Insurance premiums accrued in 2009/10:

	£
6/12 × £4,800	2,400
6/12 × £5,200	2,600
	5,000

4 Rental losses are generally carried forward against future net rental profits. However if they arise from qualifying holiday accommodation they can be set against other income in the year of the loss and/or in the preceding year.

5 The income qualifies as relevant earnings. Primarily this gives scope for relief for pension contributions.

6

	£
Rental income (£4,000 × 9/12)	3,000
Less: bad debt (£4,000 × 1/12)	(333)
expenses	(1,000)
Net rental income	1,667

Rent of £5,000 paid 4 April 2010 accrues in 2010/11 and is therefore taxed in that year.

7 B

£4,250

Chapter 4: Taxable income

1

	Non-savings income	Savings income	Dividend income
Employment income	√		
Dividend received			√
Property income	√		
Bank interest		√	
Pension income	√		
Interest on government stock		√	

2

(a) Building society interest (× 100/80) = £300

(b) Interest received on individual savings account = £nil (exempt)

(c) Dividends (× 100/90) = £160

3

	Non-savings income	Dividend income	Total
	£	£	£
Employment income	30,000		
Dividends (× 100/90)		300	
Total income	30,000	300	30,300
Less: personal allowance	(6,475)		
Taxable income	23,525	300	23,825

Interest on National Savings Certificates is exempt from income tax.

4

	Non-savings income £	Savings income £	Total £
Property income	3,000		
Building society interest			
(7,200 × 100/80)		9,000	
Total income	3,000	9,000	12,000
Less: personal allowance	(3,000)	(3,475)	
Taxable income	NIL	5,525	5,525

The personal allowance is deducted first from non-savings income and then from savings income.

5

	Non-savings income £	Savings income £	Dividend income £	Total £
Business profits	20,000			
Interest (× 100/80)		5,000		
Dividends (× 100/90)			4,000	
Total income	20,000	5,000	4,000	29,000
Less: personal allowance	(6,475)			
Taxable income	13,525	5,000	4,000	22,525

6 C

	Non-savings Income £	Savings income £	Dividend income £	Total £
Pension income	18,380			
Building society interest		5,000		
(× 100/80)				
Dividends (× 100/90)			6,000	
Total income	18,380	5,000	6,000	29,380

	£
Total income	29,380
Less: income limit	(22,900)
Excess	6,480

	£
Age allowance	9,640
Less: half excess	(3,240)
	6,400
But cannot be less than	6,475

7 B

	£
Total income	24,500
Less: Gift aid donation	(1,000)
Adjusted total income	23,500
Less: income limit	(22,900)
Excess	600

	£
Age allowance	9,490
Less: half excess	(300)
Adjusted age allowance	9,190

Chapter 5: Calculation of income tax

1 D

20% and 40%

2

	Non-savings income £	Savings income £	Dividend income £	Total £
Total income	12,000	2,000	3,000	17,000
Less: personal allowance	(6,475)	–	–	
Taxable income	5,525	2,000	3,000	10,525

Tax on non-savings income	£
£5,525 × 20%	1,105.00
Tax on savings income	
£2,000 × 20%	400.00
Tax on dividend income	
£3,000 × 10%	300.00
Tax liability	1,805.00

The £3,000 of dividend income falls within the basic rate band so is taxed at 10%.

3

	Non-savings income £	Savings income £	Dividend income £	Total £
Employment income	4,000			
Interest (× 100/80)		18,000		
Dividends (× 100/90)			22,000	
Total income	4,000	18,000	22,000	44,000
Less: personal allowance	(4,000)	(2,475)		
Taxable income	–	15,525	22,000	37,525

Tax on savings income

£2,440 × 10%	244.00
£13,085 × 20%	2,617.00
£15,525	

Tax on dividend income

£21,875 × 10%	2,187.50
£125 × 32.5%	40.62
£22,000	
Income tax liability	5,089.12

4 Basic rate tax relief is obtained by paying Gift Aid donations net of 20% tax. Additional relief is given by extending the basic rate band by the gross amount of the Gift Aid donation.

5

	Non-savings income £	Savings income £	Dividend income £	Total £
Pension income	17,000			
Property income	3,500			
Interest (received gross)		380		
Dividends (× 100/90)			700	
Total income	20,500	380	700	21,58
Less: personal allowance	(9,640)			
Taxable income	10,860	380	700	11,94

Premium bond prizes are exempt from income tax.

	£
Tax on non-savings income	
£10,860 × 20%	2,172.00
Tax on savings income	
£380 × 20%	76.00
Tax on dividend income	
£700 × 10%	70.00
	2,318.00
Less: tax suffered at source	
tax credit on dividends	(70.00)
tax deducted from employment income	(2,100.00)
Tax payable	148.00

6

	Non-savings income £	Savings income £	Dividend income £	Total £
Business profits	38,000			
Building society interest (× 100/80)		5,000		
Dividends (× 100/90)			4,000	
Total income	38,000	5,000	4,000	47,000
Less: personal allowance	(6,475)			
Taxable income	31,525	5,000	4,000	40,525

	£
Tax on non-savings income	
£31,525 × 20%	6,305.00
Tax on savings income	
£5,000 × 20%	1,000.00
Tax on dividend income	
£875 × 10%	87.50
£2,000 (extended) × 10%	200.00
£1,125 × 32.5%	365.62
	7,958.12
Less: tax credit on dividends	(400.00)
tax suffered on interest	(1,000.00)
Tax payable	6,558.12

Chapter 6: Self-assessment of income tax

1   31 January 2011

2   Payments on account of income tax for 2009/10 are due on:

   31 January 2010 and 31 July 2010

   Each payment on account due is equal to 50% of the prior year's (2008/09) income tax payable

3   £100 penalty (maximum) for failure to deliver return on time.

   5% surcharge on tax paid late. Interest on tax paid late.

4 D

28 January 2012. A year after the actual filing date because Sase filed the return before the due filing date (31 January 2011).

5 £6,000 31 January 2010

£6,000 31 July 2010

£4,000 31 January 2011

6 0

No surcharges are due on late payments on account.

Chapter 7: Computing capital gains tax

1 Both disposals are chargeable disposals.

2

	£
Proceeds	560,000
Less: cost	(325,000)
Chargeable gain	235,000

3 A

	£
Proceeds	38,000
Less: costs of disposal	(3,000)
Less: £41,500 × $\dfrac{38,000}{38,000 + 48,000}$	(18,337)
Chargeable gain	16,663

4

	£
Gains	171,000
Less: current year losses	(5,300)
	165,700
Less: losses b/f	(10,000)
	155,700
Less: annual exempt amount	(10,100)
Taxable gains	145,600

There are no losses to carry forward.

5

	£
Chargeable gains	23,800
Less: annual exemption	(10,100)
Taxable gains	13,700
CGT on £13,700 @ 18%	2,466

6 False. A loss on a disposal to a connected person can be set only against gains arising on disposals to the same connected person.

7 True. No gain or loss arises on a disposal to a spouse/civil partner.

Chapter 8: Chattels and private residences

1 (a) There is no gain or loss as the chattel is sold for gross proceeds of less than £6,000.

   (b)

	£
Net proceeds	8,200
Less: cost	(3,500)
	4,700

   Gain cannot exceed 5/3 (8,420 – 6,000) = £4,033

   Therefore, gain is £4,033.

2 0. A racehorse is an exempt asset, so no chargeable gain or allowable loss arises.

3

	£
Deemed proceeds	6,000
Less: cost	(7,000)
Allowable loss	(1,000)

4 C

   36 months

5 (a) Periods of up to three years. Where a period of absence exceeds three years, three years out of the longer period are deemed to be a period of occupation.

   (b) Periods during which the owner was required by his employment to live abroad.

   (c) Period of up to four years where the owner was:

   (i) Self-employed and forced to work away from home (UK and abroad);

   (ii) Employed and required to work elsewhere in the UK (overseas employment is covered by (b) above).

6

	£
Sale proceeds	180,000
Less: cost	(60,000)
Gain	120,000

Principal private residence exemption

	Exempt months	Chargeable months
1 April 1992 to 9 August 1995 (actual occupation)	40	
10 August 1995 to 9 August 1999 (employed abroad)	48	
10 August 1999 to 1 May 2001 (actual occupation)	21	
2 May 2001 to 30 November 2006		67
1 December 2006 to 30 November 2009 (last 36 months)	36	—
	145	67

Exempt 145/212 × £120,000 = £82,075

Gain £(120,000 – 82,075) = £37,925

Chapter 9: Shares

1 D

	No of shares	Cost £
8.91 Acquisition	10,000	5,000
4.06 Acquisition	10,000	16,000
	20,000	21,000
11.09 Disposal	(15,000)	(15,750)
c/f	5,000	5,250

	£
Proceeds of sale	30,000
Less: allowable cost	(15,750)
Chargeable gain	14,250

2 False. In a rights issue shares are paid for and this amount is added to the original cost. In a bonus issue shares are not paid for and so there is no adjustment to the original cost.

3

	No of shares	Cost £
5.00 Acquisition	2,000	12,000
12.01 1 for 2 rights issue @ £7.50	1,000	7,500
	3,000	19,500
3.10 Disposal	(2,500)	(16,250)
c/f	500	3,250

	£
Proceeds of sale	20,000
Less: allowable costs	(16,250)
Chargeable gain	3,750

INDEX

Accommodation
  expenses connected with, 24;
  job related, 26
  provision by employer, 22
Age allowance, 58
Allowable losses, 92
Annual exempt amount, 91
Asset benefit
  acquisition by employee, 18
  private use, 18
Awards: long service, 27
  staff suggestion, 27

Balancing payment, 81
Basic rate band, 66
Benefits
  exempt, 26
  taxable, 14
Bonus shares, 115

Capital gains tax, 2
Car
  company, 15
  parking space at or near work, 26
  pool, 18
  use of own for business, 24
Case law, 4
Chargeable assets, 88
Chargeable disposal, 88
Chargeable person, 88
Chattels, 102
Childcare, 27
Confidentiality, 5
Connected persons, 94
Contract for services, 12
Contract of service, 12
Costs
  acquisition, 90
  disposal, 89
  original purchase price, 90

Disclosure of information to HMRC, 6
Disposal consideration, 89
Dividend income, 55

Earnings
  receipts basis, 13
Employment, 12
Enhancement expenditure, 90
Enquiries, 83
Entertainment
  staff, 27
Exempt disposal, 88
Exempt income, 55
Expenses
  entertaining, 30
  personal incidental, 26
  reimbursement, 30
  removal, 27; subsistence, 30
  travel, 29
Extra-statutory concessions, 4

Filing due date, 76
Fuel benefit, 17

Gift Aid donation, 68
Guidelines on Professional Ethics, 5

Her Majesty's Revenue and
  Customs, 2
Higher rate threshold, 66
Home-working, 27

Income tax, 2
Individual savings account (ISA), 55
Interest on late paid tax, 82

Listed shares, 116
Loan
  beneficial to employees, 19

Matching rules, 112
Material error or omission in tax
    return, 6
Mobile phone, 28
Money laundering, 7

National Savings and Investments,
    56
No gain/no loss disposal, 94
Non-savings income, 54

P11D employees, 15
Part disposal, 90
Payment on account, 80
Payroll deduction scheme, 29
Penalties
    failure to keep records, 80
    for error, 77
    late filing, 79
    late notification, 79
Pensions, 28
Personal allowance, 58
Principal Private Residence, 104
Property income
    accruals basis, 40
    definition, 40
    losses, 45
    qualifying holiday accomodation,
    45
    rent-a-room relief, 46
    renwals basis, 44
    wear and tear allowance, 44

Records, 2, 77
Repayment supplement, 83
Revenue and Customs Briefs, 4
Rights issue, 115

Savings income, 54
Savings income starting rate band, 67
Self employment, 12
Share pool, 112
Spouses/civil partners, 94
Statements of practice, 4
Statue law, 3
Statutory mileage rate scheme, 25
Surcharges, 82

Tax payable, 70
Tax year, 2
Taxable gains, 91
Taxable income, 58
Total income, 57
Travel: business, 30

Unlisted shares, 116

Van benefit, 18
Vouchers: cash, 24
    childcare, 27
    meal, 26

Wasting chattel, 102
Work related training, 27

Notes

Notes

REVIEW FORM

How have you used this Text?
(Tick one box only)

☐ Home study

☐ On a course_____

☐ Other _____

Why did you decide to purchase this Text? *(Tick one box only)*

☐ Have used BPP Texts in the past

☐ Recommendation by friend/colleague

☐ Recommendation by a college lecturer

☐ Saw advertising

☐ Other _____

During the past six months do you recall seeing/receiving either of the following?
(Tick as many boxes as are relevant)

☐ Our advertisement in Accounting Technician

☐ Our Publishing Catalogue

Which (if any) aspects of our advertising do you think are useful?
(Tick as many boxes as are relevant)

☐ Prices and publication dates of new editions

☐ Information on Text content

☐ Details of our free online offering

☐ None of the above

Your ratings, comments and suggestions would be appreciated on the following areas of this Text.

	Very useful	Useful	Not useful
Introductory section	☐	☐	☐
Quality of explanations	☐	☐	☐
How it works	☐	☐	☐
Chapter tasks	☐	☐	☐
Chapter Overviews	☐	☐	☐
Test your learning	☐	☐	☐
Index	☐	☐	☐

	Excellent	Good	Adequate	Poor
Overall opinion of this Text	☐	☐	☐	☐

Do you intend to continue using BPP Products? ☐ Yes ☐ No

Please note any further comments and suggestions/errors on the reverse of this page. The author of this edition can be e-mailed at: suedexter@bpp.com

Please return to: Sue Dexter, Publishing Director, BPP Learning Media Ltd, FREEPOST, London, W12 8BR.

Please note any further comments and suggestions/errors below.

Paul.   (12th → 19th March)

→ Gemma - 3rd March + 17th March - can't do.
10th

→ Nina - 31st March